BRITISH
WARSHIPS
...RIES

FORT VICTORIA
LONDON
A387

• NICK NEWNS   **HM Ships Exeter, Cornwall and RFA Fort Victoria**

THE ROYAL NAVY

In July 2008, almost a decade after the government placed the Future Aircraft Carrier programme at the heart of its 1998 Strategic Defence Review (SDR), the MoD finally put pen to paper and signed the production contract for two aircraft carriers. Originally conceived as 40,000 ton vessels, HMS QUEEN ELIZABETH and HMS PRINCE OF WALES have evolved into 65,000 ton giants. To be delivered in 2014 and 2016 respectively, these two vessels are the long awaited cornerstone of the SDR - a paper that promised the RN the biggest shipbuilding programme since the end of the Second World War. But ten years on has SDR delivered what it promised for the RN?

Since 1998 much has changed on the world stage. The terror attacks on the World Trade centre in the US, the public transport systems in the UK and Spain and the bombing of tourists in Bali, brought terror group Al Qaeda to the fore. The need to combat the growing terror threat has embroiled the UK in the Global War on Terror - a coalition effort to rid the world of the Al Qaeda menace. The UK has now been fighting this war in both Iraq and Afghanistan for many years with no sign of an end. The war is a constant drain on manpower material and resources. The requirement to replace vulnerable land vehicles has seen a massive acquisition programme to provide mine resistant and ambush protected vehicles as urgent operational requirements. Both Harrier aircraft and helicopters are being heavily used in support of the troops on the ground and there are real concerns over the lack of helicopter lift and the rapid rate at which present rotary lift (and tactical fixed wing transport) are wearing out. All of this sustained fighting tempo is draining already scarce resources.

As money becomes even tighter the MoD reported in 2008 that the emphasis on procurement and funding should be prioritised - the priority switching to current operations, meaning that the bulk of any funds will find their way to supporting the fighting in the sandpits of Iraq and Afghanistan.

As if this was not going to put enough of a squeeze on an already dwindling pot of cash for the RN, 2008 also witnessed a worldwide financial crash, with the banking system seemingly in freefall and the UK government borrowing billions of pounds to shore up the banking infrastructure in an attempt to stop the total collapse of the economy.

In 2009, it will be against this backdrop that the RN will be fighting for funding and survival of its procurement programmes. SDR, which promised much for the RN, has delivered very little. SDR was intended to reshape the armed forces from a cold war footing into a force capable of expeditionary warfare on a global scale, the emphasis of which would be on rapidly deployable forces capable of global power projection with the ability to deploy offensive air power in support of military intervention in the littoral areas. It is perhaps worthwhile to look at some of these proposed new programmes, designed to achieve this, in a little more detail.

Without doubt, the RN has gained particularly with regard to amphibious capability. The requirement for rapid worldwide deployment of troops and equipment by sea saw the acquisition of six Ro-Ro vessels, civilian operated, but at the disposal of the MoD to deliver vehicles, equipment and stores to operational theatres. These are backed up by the four Bay class LSD(A)s which can transport and land both troops and equipment, while sitting offshore to support them once in theatre. The command and control aspects, as well as aviation support are provided by OCEAN, ALBION and BULWARK. This is perhaps the single success story to have emerged from SDR so far and there can be little doubt that the RN/RFA now provide a highly capable and modern sealift capability.

The aircraft carriers were to be the cornerstone of the SDR, being able to project power from the sea - a crucial capability for any littoral actions. Though the gestation period for these vessels was long and convoluted, they remained key to the SDR, the government concluding that they cannot be certain that the UK will always have access to suitable air bases or that even when they do, experience has shown that bases may not always be available in the early stages of a crisis, and that their infrastructure is not always able to support the full range of operations required. The aircraft carriers therefore are now to be a reality, with construction scheduled to begin in 2009. But under the current financial climate, are they safe? Being built in the Prime Minister's backyard and with thousands of shipbuilding jobs at stake it seems fairly certain, that whilst this goverment are in power, the carriers will be completed. What is far from certain is what aircraft they will eventually operate. The increasingly complex and expensive F-35B Lightning is still not a certainty. Although the government have committed to the research and development of this aircraft, there are still too many unanswered questions. Key amongst these is why do the RN need a vertical take-off aircraft when they will be operating from a large deck carrier. Without a catapult or arrestor gear, these 65,000 ton giants will not be able to operate fixed wing Airborne Early Warning aircraft, or an aircraft capable of refuelling its own air wing. Of greater significance, it will not be able to support or operate aircraft from the USN or France, significantly reducing its effectiveness when operating within a coalition. The MoD are investigating rolling landings for the F-35B in order to give a significant bring home weight (ie not having to ditch unspent fuel or unused ordinance prior to landing). Rolling landings without arrestor gear are fraught with danger and one wonders why the MoD aren't looking at acquiring the F-35C variant - designed for operation from a large deck carrier, or the FA-18 Hornet - a far cheaper and perhaps more versatile aircraft. The fact that the MoD have not yet contracted for the construction of hull blocks above hangar deck on the carriers suggests that they are not yet ready to reveal their hand.

SDR gave a firm commitment to maintaining a destroyer/frigate force of 32 ships. Initially, the Type 42 destroyer was to be replaced by up to 12 Type 45 destroyers. This was quickly reduced to up to eight and in 2008 it was finally confirmed that the RN would get only six of these ships. The MoD argument that they are far more capable vessels than originally expected, does not seem to factor in that they can only be deployed in one place at a time. It must also be noted that though they are indeed vastly more capable than the ships which they replace, they are in fact significantly *less* capable than they were first designed - close in weapon systems and Harpoon missiles being a 'fitted for, but not with' capability.

The Future Surface Combatant (FSC) programme was intended to start replacing the current frigate force in 2012 (the first vessel to be replaced, SHEFFIELD, now long since decommissioned). In June 2008 it was announced that with the reduction of the Type 45 programme to just six ships, the FSC programme would be brought forward to deliver the first ship by 2019.

Today the destroyer/frigate force stands at just 25 ships. Once the Type 45s are in service this number will be just 23. With FSC not expected to deliver until 2019 this could reduce to just 20-22 ships by then. These few vessels, of which up to a third can be expected to be in maintenance at any one time, will be expected to conduct all RN standing tasks while also undertaking escort duty of the RNs high value, relatively unprotected, aircraft carriers and amphibious ships (9 ships). In November 2008 the MoD announced revised decommissioning dates for the Type 23 and Type 22 frigates, keeping them in operation for up to 35 years. This should be good news for the dockyards as these ships are likely to require some form of service life extension programme.

The submarine service is also faring badly. Quoted within the SDR as being "an extremely potent weapon system with an important role to play in support of a wide range of operations," the Tomahawk equipped SSN force was to be reduced from 12 to 10 boats. In fact following delays to the Astute class and a lack of follow-on orders, the SSN force is due to drop to just eight submarines and may well settle at seven. To date there are only four Astute class on order and despite the government statement that SSN production would achieve a 'drumbeat' of one submarine every 22 months, their commitment to a replacement Trident submarine programme could place even this in jeopardy. A recent National Audit Office report has stated that for the Trident replacement programme to achieve its stated in service date, construction work would have to commence in 2014. With the Astute programme ongoing one has to ask if the facilities at BAE SYSTEMS at Barrow, could cope with building two submarine classes simultaneously. One thing is sure - more Astute class need to be ordered soon if fleet numbers, and the drumbeat of 22 months, are to be achieved.

At SDR the mine countermeasures force comprised 25 vessels which was reduced to 22 (11 Hunt and 11 Sandown class). This was subsequently reviewed and reduced once more to just 16 ships (eight of each). At a time when port and border security are so important, a dedicated and capable MCM force would seem to be essential. In fact the RN has deployed four MCMs to the Gulf, providing long term port security and clear sea access in the region. Others have operationally deployed to the Baltic to provide clear access to Baltic ports. The reasoning behind the MCM force reduction is hard to fathom in the current climate, but might have been influenced by the trend to move away from dedicated MCM assets to more portable systems capable of deployment from a large range of ships. However, this still leaves a gap in the number of small vessels available to provide presence and security around UK ports.

Not to be forgotten are the vessels that support the RN on deployed operations. The Royal Fleet Auxiliary has now been reduced to just 16 vessels of which only six are dedicated tankers and a further four ships capable of transferring both fuel and solid stores.

The future of the RFA lies with the Maritime Afloat and Sustainability (MARS) programme and a proposed fleet of up to eleven vessels to be delivered by 2021. The first part of the programme for up to six tankers is already seeking tenders and might see the ships built abroad, although an eleventh hour partnering arrangement between one of the bidders, Fincantieri and Northwestern Shiprepairers and Shipbuilders (NSL) may yet see some of the vessels built at Birkenhead.

While the RN and MoD struggle to bring its new programmes and ships into service, the RN is also facing a problem with its public profile. Many in the press and government argue that the RN needs more ships and greater capability, one has to ask how the RN would man them if they were to get them.

The RN has always suffered from the fact that much of its work is done over the horizon and out of the public eye - as a result its public profile is that much smaller than those of the other two services. This despite the fact that much of its work involves contributes directly to the UK such as counter-drugs operations in the Caribbean and Gulf and more recently anti-piracy operations off Somalia. Likewise, public perception is that the war in the sandpits is an Army and RAF operation. How wrong they are. In 2008 RN personnel in Afghanistan comprised the majority of deployed forces with Royal Marine Commandos, Royal Navy support personnel driving vehicles and providing medical facilities; RN pilots flying Harriers and much of the rotary helicopter lift being provided by RN helicopters. With everyone dressed in combat kit it is hard to tell the services apart. There is, it seems, a move to return the services back to their own uniforms, thereby giving them back some of their own corporate identity - it can't come soon enough.

With Navy Days now only taking place every two years, the chances of the public getting to meet the RN are becoming more and more remote. Without exposing the youngsters of the day to the RN experience you have to wonder how the service is going to entice people into joining up. I was fortunate enough to go to sea with the RN for Staff College Sea Days last autumn - an event where the RN presents its capabilities to students at the Staff College, both UK and overseas. As the assembled ships sailed from harbour and threw themselves around the ocean to avoid attack from fast missile boats and low level air attack, then followed it up with refuelling from a tanker, I couldn't help wondering whether this sort of shop window would be just a good for attracting potential recruits - invited school parties replacing staff college students for a couple of days - I dare say Health and Safety would have something to say about it! The fact remains that unless the RN can attract young people into the service - and more importantly, retain those that it has, there is little point bemoaning the ever shrinking size of the fleet. The bottom line is that without manpower, you can't man the ships and if you can't man the ships, there is little point in having them.

There are uncertain times ahead for the RN in 2009/10 with the need to tighten national spending. With large high cost programmes in the early stages of production or planning the potential for cancellation is never far away and the RN remain vulnerable to further defence cuts.

Steve Bush
December 2008

6

SHIPS OF THE ROYAL NAVY
Pennant Numbers

Ship	Pennant Number	Page	Ship	Pennant Number	Page
Aircraft Carriers			CORNWALL	F99	21
			LANCASTER	F229	19
INVINCIBLE	R05	13	ARGYLL	F231	19
ILLUSTRIOUS	R06	13	IRON DUKE	F234	19
ARK ROYAL	R07	13	MONMOUTH	F235	19
			MONTROSE	F236	19
Assault Ships			WESTMINSTER	F237	19
			NORTHUMBERLAND	F238	19
OCEAN	L12	14	RICHMOND	F239	19
ALBION	L14	15			
BULWARK	L15	15	**Submarines**		
			VANGUARD	S28	9
Destroyers			VICTORIOUS	S29	9
			VIGILANT	S30	9
DARING	D32	16	VENGEANCE	S31	9
EXETER •	D89	17	TURBULENT	S87	11
SOUTHAMPTON •	D90	17	TIRELESS	S88	11
NOTTINGHAM •	D91	17	TORBAY	S90	11
LIVERPOOL	D92	17	TRENCHANT	S91	11
MANCHESTER	D95	18	TALENT	S92	11
GLOUCESTER	D96	18	TRIUMPH	S93	11
EDINBURGH	D97	18	SCEPTRE	S104	12
YORK	D98	18	TRAFALGAR	S107	11
• Ship at Extended Readiness			ASTUTE	S119	10
Frigates			**Minehunters**		
KENT	F78	19			
PORTLAND	F79	19	LEDBURY	M30	22
SUTHERLAND	F81	19	CATTISTOCK	M31	22
SOMERSET	F82	19	BROCKLESBY	M33	22
ST ALBANS	F83	19	MIDDLETON	M34	22
CUMBERLAND	F85	21	CHIDDINGFOLD	M37	22
CAMPBELTOWN	F86	21	ATHERSTONE	M38	22
CHATHAM	F87	21	HURWORTH	M39	22

Ship	Pennant Number	Page	Ship	Pennant Number	Page
QUORN	M41	22	RAIDER	P275	27
WALNEY	M104	23	BLAZER	P279	27
PENZANCE	M106	23	DASHER	P280	27
PEMBROKE	M107	23	TYNE	P281	24
GRIMSBY	M108	23	SEVERN	P282	24
BANGOR	M109	23	MERSEY	P283	24
RAMSEY	M110	23	SCIMITAR	P284	26
BLYTH	M111	23	SABRE	P285	26
SHOREHAM	M112	23	PUNCHER	P291	27
			CHARGER	P292	27
Patrol Craft			RANGER	P293	27
			TRUMPETER	P294	27
EXPRESS	P163	27			
EXPLORER	P164	27	**Survey Ships & RN**		
EXAMPLE	P165	27	**Manned Auxiliaries**		
EXPLOIT	P167	27			
CLYDE	P257	25	GLEANER	H86	32
ARCHER	P264	27	ECHO	H87	30
BITER	P270	27	ENTERPRISE	H88	30
SMITER	P272	27	ROEBUCK	H130	31
PURSUER	P273	27	SCOTT	H131	29
TRACKER	P274	27	ENDURANCE	A171	33

8

HMS Vigilant

VANGUARD CLASS

Ship	Pennant Number	Completion Date	Builder
VANGUARD	S28	1992	VSEL
VICTORIOUS	S29	1994	VSEL
VIGILANT	S30	1997	VSEL
VENGEANCE	S31	1999	VSEL

Displacement 15,000 tons (dived) **Dimensions** 150m x 13m x 12m **Speed** 25 + dived **Armament** 16 - Trident 2 (D5) missiles, 4 Torpedo Tubes **Complement** 132

Notes

After the first successful UK D5 missile firing in May '94 the first operational patrol was carried out in early '95 and a patrol has been constantly maintained ever since. The UK's Trident missiles have been de-targeted since 1994, and the submarine on deterrent patrol is normally at several days notice to fire her missiles. The submarines have two crews each to maintain the maximum period on patrol. VICTORIOUS completed a three-year refit at Devonport in 2008. VIGILANT, the third vessel to enter the refit cycle, arrived at Devonport on 11 October 2008. In 2007 the Government announced its intention to retain the submarine-based deterrent and studies into a successor to the Trident fleet are underway.

9

HMS Astute

ASTUTE CLASS

Ship	Pennant Number	Completion Date	Builder
ASTUTE	S119	2009	BAE Submarine Solutions
AMBUSH	S120	Building	BAE Submarine Solutions
ARTFUL	S121	Building	BAE Submarine Solutions
AUDACIOUS	S122	Building	BAE Submarine Solutions

Displacement 7,000 tonnes (7,800 dived) **Dimensions** 97m x 11.3m x 10.0m
Speed 29+ dived **Armament** 6 Torpedo Tubes; Tomahawk cruise missiles **Complement** 84 (Accommodation for 12 Officers and 97 Ratings.)

Notes

Ordered in 1997, the Astute class were intended, initially, to replace the S class in RN service. The initial history of the programme was one of severe overspend and delays, leading in 2003 to a restructuring of the entire contract. The programme is now back on track with the first vessel, ASTUTE, launched on 8 June 2007. Sea trials planned for 2008 were delayed by repair work. After nuclear-fuel was loaded into the reactor the submarine was "re-launched" from Devonshire Hall in October 2008. Sea Trials now expected to commence in 2009 after which the submarine will move to Faslane for defect rectification.
To keep nuclear skills alive BAE have stated that an order every 22 months is essential to maintain a 'drumbeat' of production. AMBUSH is scheduled to launched in 2009.

HMS Tireless

TRAFALGAR CLASS

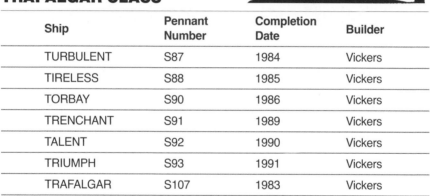

Ship	Pennant Number	Completion Date	Builder
TURBULENT	S87	1984	Vickers
TIRELESS	S88	1985	Vickers
TORBAY	S90	1986	Vickers
TRENCHANT	S91	1989	Vickers
TALENT	S92	1990	Vickers
TRIUMPH	S93	1991	Vickers
TRAFALGAR	S107	1983	Vickers

Displacement 4,500 tons **Dimensions** 85m x 10m x 8m **Speed** 30+ dived **Armament** 5 Torpedo Tubes; Tomahawk cruise missiles **Complement** 110.

Notes

Quieter, faster and with greater endurance than the Swiftsure class. Tomahawk Cruise Missiles are fitted in TRIUMPH, TRAFALGAR, TURBULENT and TRENCHANT. It is expected Tomahawk will eventually be fitted in all of these boats. TURBULENT returned to the fleet in 2008 following a 15-month refit at Devonport. TRIUMPH will start post-refit trials in the Summer and return to the fleet in 2010. Decommissioning dates are: TRAFALGAR (2009); TURBULENT (2011); TIRELESS (2013); TORBAY (2015); TRENCHANT (2017); TALENT (2019) and TRIUMPH (2022).

HMS Sceptre

SWIFTSURE CLASS

Ship	Pennant Number	Completion Date	Builder
SCEPTRE	S104	1978	Vickers

Displacement 4,500 tons dived **Dimensions** 83m x 10m x 8m **Speed** 30 knots + dived **Armament** 5 Torpedo Tubes, Tomahawk cruise missiles **Complement** 116.

Notes

SCEPTRE entered the shiplift at Faslane in 2008 as the last Swiftsure class submarine to undergo a 37-week Revalidation Assisted Maintenance Period (RAMP). Work was scheduled to be completed in January. SUPERB decommissioned on 26 September 2008 at Devonport, where she returned following a grounding in the Red Sea. She joins her sisters SPARTAN, SPENDID and SOVEREIGN at Devonport, all of which are awaiting defuelling and storage afloat. SCEPTRE is scheduled to decommission in 2010.

HMS Ark Royal

INVINCIBLE CLASS

Ship	Pennant Number	Completion Date	Builder
INVINCIBLE	R05	1979	Vickers
ILLUSTRIOUS	R06	1982	Swan Hunter
ARK ROYAL	R07	1985	Swan Hunter

Displacement 22,500 tonnes **Dimensions** 210m x 36m x 6.5m **Speed** 28 knots **Armament** 2 - 20mm guns, 3 Phalanx/Goalkeeper **Aircraft** Tailored Air Group (Harrier GR9, Merlin, Sea King, Chinook as required) **Complement** 752 + 384 Air Group (600 troops in LPH role).

Notes
Only one carrier is operational at any one time. ILLUSTRIOUS assumed the role of fleet flagship in June 2005. ARK ROYAL fitted with a mizzen mast at the end of the island structure and able to operate in both the Strike Carrier or LPH role. INVINCIBLE decommissioned in July 2005 and was placed at Extended Readiness at Portsmouth until 2010 when she is likely to be put up for disposal. Vessels are now roled as Strike Carriers rather than ASW vessels and as such deploy with a Tailored Air Group to meet the specific operational needs of any deployment. ILLUSTRIOUS to deploy to Mediterranean in early 2009 as part of Taurus '09 Task Group. ARK ROYAL is to decommission in 2012 and ILLUSTRIOUS in 2015.

HMS Ocean

LANDING PLATFORM HELICOPTER (LPH)

Ship	Pennant Number	Completion Date	Builder
OCEAN	L12	1998	Kvaerner

Displacement 21,578 tonnes **Dimensions** 208m x 34m x 6.6m **Speed** 17 knots **Armament** 3 x Phalanx, 4 x 20mm BMARC guns, 4 x Minigun **Complement** Ship 284, Squadrons 180, Embarked force 600.

Notes

Can carry 12 Sea King and 6 Lynx helicopters. Frequently employed as the flagship of the UK Amphibious Ready Group. RAF Chinook helicopters are normally carried as an integral part of the ship's air group, but they are unable to be stowed below decks. Modified with two 50m blisters attached to the hull at the waterline below the after chine to improve safety margins while deploying LCVPs from the after davits. Vessel is somewhat constrained by her slow speed. She rejoined the fleet in October 2008 following a £35 million refit at Devonport. The work included improvements in accomodation for both crew and embarked Royal Marines; advanced communications facilities; a better weapon defence system and an upgrade to the ship's aviation support facilities to improve support to helicopter operations including the Apache attack helicopter.

• COR VAN NEIKERKEN

HMS Albion

LANDING PLATFORM DOCK (LPD)

ALBION CLASS

Ship	Pennant Number	Completion Date	Builder
ALBION	L14	2003	BAe Systems
BULWARK	L15	2004	BAe Systems

Displacement 18,500 tons, 21,500 tons (flooded) **Dimensions** 176m x 25.6m x 6.1m
Speed 18 knots **Armament** 2 x CIWS, 2 x 20mm guns (single) **Complement** 325
Military Lift 303 troops, with an overload capacity of a further 405.

Notes

Vehicle deck capacity for up to six Challenger 2 tanks or around 30 armoured all-terrain tracked vehicles. Floodable well dock, with the capacity to take four utility landing craft. Four smaller landing craft carried on davits, each capable of carrying 35 troops. Two-spot flight deck able to take medium support helicopters and stow a third. The Flight Deck is capable of taking the Chinook. These vessels do not have a hangar but have equipment needed to support aircraft operations. During upgrades at Devonport the ships have been converted from direct diesel drive with electric propulsion back-up to a full electrical propulsion system. ALBION entered a 10-month, £26 million refit at Devonport in October 2008.

15

DESTROYERS
DARING CLASS
(Type 45)

Ship	Pennant Number	Completion Date	Builder
DARING	D32	2008	BVT Surface Fleet
DAUNTLESS	*D33*	*Building*	*BVT Surface Fleet*
DIAMOND	*D34*	*Building*	*BVT Surface Fleet*
DRAGON	*D35*	*Building*	*BVT Surface Fleet*
DEFENDER	*D36*	*Building*	*BVT Surface Fleet*
DUNCAN	*D37*	*Building*	*BVT Surface Fleet*

Displacement 7,350 tons **Dimensions** 152.4m x 21.2m x 5.7m **Speed** 29 knots **Armament** 1 - 4.5-inch gun, Sylver VLS with combination of up to 48 Aster 15 and Aster 30 missiles **Aircraft** Lynx or Merlin **Complement** 190 (with space for 235).

Notes
BAE and VT merged in 2008 to form BVT Surface Fleet. Originally to have been a class of up to 12 ships this has been reduced to just eight, but in 2008 it was confirmed that no more than six would be ordered. The bow sections, funnels and masts are built at Portsmouth, which are then transported by barge to Govan where final assembly and fitting out takes place. DARING completed her final set of contractor sea trials in September 2008 and was planned to be handed over to the RN in December. DAUNTLESS sailed for initial sea trials on 14 November 2008. The fourth vessel DRAGON was launched on 17 November 2008.

• DAVID HANNAFORD

HMS Liverpool

SHEFFIELD CLASS
(Type 42) Batch 2

Ship	Pennant Number	Completion Date	Builder
EXETER	D89	1980	Swan Hunter
SOUTHAMPTON	D90	1981	Vosper T.
NOTTINGHAM	D91	1982	Vosper T.
LIVERPOOL	D92	1982	C. Laird

Displacement 3,660 tons **Dimensions** 125m x 15m x 7m **Speed** 29 knots **Armament** 1 - 4.5-inch gun, 4 - 20mm guns, Sea Dart Missile System: 2 - Phalanx, Lynx Helicopter, 6 Torpedo Tubes **Complement** 266.

Notes
Barring a national emergency, NOTTINGHAM, SOUTHAMPTON and EXETER are expected to remain alongside at Portsmouth until decommissioned in 2009. Phalanx has been removed from SOUTHAMPTON and EXETER and their Sea Dart capability mothballed. According to government figures released in November 2008, EXETER and SOUTHAMPTON will decommission in 2009 and NOTTINGHAM in 2010. The sole remaining Batch 2 vessel, LIVERPOOL, is scheduled to decommission in 2012.

HMS Edinburgh

SHEFFIELD CLASS
(Type 42) Batch 3

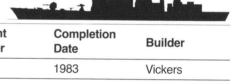

Ship	Pennant Number	Completion Date	Builder
MANCHESTER	D95	1983	Vickers
GLOUCESTER	D96	1984	Vosper T.
EDINBURGH	D97	1985	C. Laird
YORK	D98	1984	Swan Hunter

Displacement 4,775 tons **Dimensions** 132m x 15m x 7m **Speed** 30 knots + **Armament** 1- 4.5-inch gun, 2 - Phalanx, 2 - 20mm guns, Sea Dart missile system, Lynx Helicopter, 6 Torpedo Tubes **Complement** 269.

Notes
Stretched versions of earlier ships of this class. Designed to provide area defence of a task force. Deck edge stiffening fitted to counter increased hull stress. EDINBURGH and YORK (only) fitted with 4.5-inch Mod 1 gun. The following decommissioning dates were announced in Spetember 2007: MANCHESTER & GLOUCESTER (2011), YORK (2012) & EDINBURGH (2013). Vessels are now frequently seen without the distinctive radome covers over their Type 909 trackers. Despite the announcement that there will now only be six Type 45 destroyers built the intention is to decommission all of the Type 42 destroyers before the final Type 45 enters service.

HMS Kent

FRIGATES

DUKE CLASS (Type 23)

Ship	Pennant Number	Completion Date	Builder
KENT	F78	2000	Yarrow
PORTLAND	F79	2000	Yarrow
SUTHERLAND*	F81	1997	Yarrow
SOMERSET*	F82	1996	Yarrow
ST ALBANS	F83	2001	Yarrow
LANCASTER*	F229	1991	Yarrow
ARGYLL	F231	1991	Yarrow
IRON DUKE*	F234	1992	Yarrow
MONMOUTH*	F235	1993	Yarrow
MONTROSE*	F236	1993	Yarrow

Ship	Pennant Number	Completion Date	Builder
WESTMINSTER	F237	1993	Swan Hunter
NORTHUMBERLAND*	F238	1994	Swan Hunter
RICHMOND*	F239	1994	Swan Hunter

Displacement 3,500 tons **Dimensions** 133m x 15m x 5m **Speed** 28 knots **Armament** Harpoon & Seawolf missile systems: 1 - 4.5-inch gun, 2 - single 30mm guns, 4 - 2 twin, magazine launched, Torpedo Tubes, Lynx or Merlin helicopter **Complement** 173.

Notes
The ships incorporate 'Stealth' technology to minimise magnetic, radar, acoustic and infra-red signatures. Gas turbine and diesel electric propulsion. Those ships marked * have been fitted with the Mk 8 Mod 1 4.5-inch gun. The rest of class to be fitted by 2011. Type 2087 Sonar is to be fitted in only 9 of the remaining 13 of the class (ARGYLL, MONTROSE, MONMOUTH and IRON DUKE will not receive the upgrade).

In November 2008 revised decommissioning dates were announced, extending the service life of the Type 23s by up to eight years. The new decommissioning dates are as follows (old dates in brackets): ARGYLL 2023 (*2019*); LANCASTER 2024 (*2019*); IRON DUKE 2025 (*2020*); MONMOUTH 2026 (*2021*); MONTROSE 2027 (*2021*); WESTMINSTER 2028 (*2021*); NORTHUMBERLAND 2029 (*2022*); RICHMOND 2030 (*2022*); SOMERSET 2031 (*2023*); SUTHERLAND 2033 (*2025*); KENT 2034 (*2028*); PORTLAND 2035 (*2028*) and ST. ALBANS 2036 (*2029*).

HMS Cumberland

BROADSWORD CLASS
(Type 22) Batch 3

Ship	Pennant Number	Completion Date	Builder
CUMBERLAND	F85	1988	Yarrow
CAMPBELTOWN	F86	1988	C. Laird
CHATHAM	F87	1989	Swan Hunter
CORNWALL	F99	1987	Yarrow

Displacement 4,200 tons **Dimensions** 147m x 15m x 7m **Speed** 30 knots **Armament** 1 - 4.5-inch gun, 1 - Goalkeeper, 8 - Harpoon, 2 - Seawolf, 2 - 20mm guns, 6 Torpedo Tubes, 2 Lynx or 1 Sea King Helicopter **Complement** 259.

Notes

All these ships have an anti-submarine and intelligence gathering capability. All are capable of acting as fleet flagships. CUMBERLAND fitted with Mk8 4.5-inch Mod 1 gun in 2001 and the remainder will be fitted by the end of the decade. Decommissioning dates were revised in November 2008 (old dates in brackets): CORNWALL 2019 (*2015*); CAMPBELTOWN 2020 (*2017*); CUMBERLAND 2021(*2017*) and CHATHAM 2022 (*2018*).

21

HMS Hurworth

MINE COUNTERMEASURES SHIPS (MCMV) HUNT CLASS

Ship	Pennant Number	Completion Date	Builder
LEDBURY	M30	1981	Vosper T.
CATTISTOCK	M31	1982	Vosper T.
BROCKLESBY	M33	1983	Vosper T.
MIDDLETON	M34	1984	Yarrow
CHIDDINGFOLD	M37	1984	Vosper T.
ATHERSTONE	M38	1987	Vosper T.
HURWORTH	M39	1985	Vosper T.
QUORN	M41	1989	Vosper T.

Displacement 625 tonnes **Dimensions** 60m x 10m x 2.2m **Speed** 17 knots **Armament** 1 x 30mm + 2 x 20mm guns **Complement** 42.

Notes

The largest warships ever built of glass reinforced plastic. Their cost (£35m each) has dictated the size of the class. Very sophisticated ships - and lively seaboats! All are based at Portsmouth as the Second Mine Countermeasures Squadron (MCM2). The Fishery Protection role was relinquished in 2008. LEDBURY to decommission in 2019, CATTISTOCK, BROCKLESBY, CHIDDINGFOLD and MIDDLETON 2020, HURWORTH and ATHERSTONE 2022 and QUORN 2023. In order to keep up the deployment tempo, crews can be swapped between ship. The decommissioned BRECON is a Seamanship Training Vessel attached to the New Entry Training Establishment, HMS RALEIGH, at Torpoint.

• ANTHONY VELLA

HMS Walney

SANDOWN CLASS

Ship	Pennant Number	Completion Date	Builder
WALNEY	M104	1992	Vosper T.
PENZANCE	M106	1998	Vosper T.
PEMBROKE	M107	1998	Vosper T.
GRIMSBY	M108	1999	Vosper T.
BANGOR	M109	2000	Vosper T.
RAMSEY	M110	2000	Vosper T.
BLYTH	M111	2001	Vosper T.
SHOREHAM	M112	2001	Vosper T.

Displacement 450 tons **Dimensions** 53m x 10m x 2m **Speed** 13 knots
Armament 1 - 30mm gun **Complement** 34.

Notes

A class dedicated to a single mine hunting role. Propulsion is by vectored thrust and bow thrusters. All are based at Faslane as the First Mine Countermeasures Squadron (MCM1). PEMBROKE and GRIMSBY sailed from Faslane in October 2008 for a two year deployment to the Gulf. They relieved BLYTH and RAMSEY who had left the UK in 2006. The decommissioned CROMER is a static training hull (renamed HINDUSTAN) at Dartmouth.   Three transferred to the Estonian Navy - ADMIRAL COWAN (ex-SANDOWN) delivered in 2007. SAKALA (ex-INVERNESS) delivered in January 2008 and UGALA (ex-BRIDORT) in 2009.

HMS Mersey

PATROL VESSELS

RIVER CLASS

Ship	Pennant Number	Completion Date	Builder
TYNE	P281	2002	Vosper T.
SEVERN	P282	2003	Vosper T.
MERSEY	P283	2003	Vosper T.

Displacement 1700 tonnes **Dimensions** 80m x 13.5m x 3.8m **Speed** 20+ knots **Armament** 1 x 20mm, 2 x GPMG **Complement** 48

Notes

Ordered on 8 May 2001, the deal was unusual in that the ships are being leased from Vospers (VT) for five years under a £60 million contract. Thereafter the opportunity exists for the lease to be extended, the ships purchased outright or returned to VT. So far the arrangement seems to have been a success with VT meeting their commitment of having the ships available for over 300 days a year. In January 2007 a £52 million lease-contract extension was awarded extending their RN service to the end of 2013. The River class are now the only RN ships conducting Fishery Protection patrols in the waters around England, Wales and Northern Ireland .

• NICK NEWNS

HMS Clyde

BATCH II RIVER CLASS

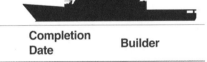

Ship	Pennant Number	Completion Date	Builder
CLYDE	P257	2006	VT Shipbuilding

Displacement 1,850 tons **Dimensions** 81.5m x 13.6m x 3.8m **Speed** 19 knots (full load) 21 knots (sprint) **Aircraft** Flight Deck to take Lynx, Sea King or Merlin Helicopter **Armament** 1 - 30mm gun **Complement** 36 (space for additional 20 personnel)

Notes
Designed to carry out patrol duties around the Falklands and their dependencies, the ship is able to accommodate a single helicopter up to Merlin size. CLYDE was launched from Vosper Thornycroft's Portsmouth facility on 20 June 2006 and accepted into service on 31 October. She deployed to the Falklands in August 2007. It is envisaged that CLYDE's more modern design will enable her to remain on task in the South Atlantic until 2012. Like the previous River class, she has been leased from the VT Group, for a period of five years.

HMS Scimitar

LIFESPAN PATROL VESSELS (LPVs)

Ship	Pennant Number	Completion Date	Builder
SCIMITAR	P284	1988	Halmatic
SABRE	P285	1988	Halmatic

Displacement 18.5 tons   **Dimensions** 16m x 4.7m x 1.4m   **Speed** 27+ knots
Armament 2 x GPMG **Complement** 4

Notes
Purpose built in 1988 for counter terrorism duties on Lough Neagh, Northern Ireland. Operated in anonimity until withdrawn from service in 2002, following a review of RN operations in the Province. Transferred to Gibraltar in September 2002 to join the Gibraltar Patrol Boat Squadron. On completion of trials they were commissioned on 31 January 2003 and renamed SCIMITAR (ex-GREYFOX) and SABRE (ex-GREY-WOLF). Tasked with ensuring the security and integrity of British Gibraltar Territorial Waters (BGTW), the Squadron is permanently assigned to the Operational Command of Commander Joint Operations.

HMS Ranger

COASTAL TRAINING CRAFT
P2000 CLASS

Ship	Pennant Number	Completion Date	Builder
EXPRESS	P163	1988	Vosper T.
EXPLORER	P164	1985	Watercraft
EXAMPLE	P165	1985	Watercraft
EXPLOIT	P167	1988	Vosper T.
ARCHER	P264	1985	Watercraft
BITER	P270	1985	Watercraft
SMITER	P272	1986	Watercraft
PURSUER	P273	1988	Vosper T.

Ship	Pennant Number	Completion Date	Builder
TRACKER	P274	1998	Ailsa Troon
RAIDER	P275	1998	Ailsa Troon
BLAZER	P279	1988	Vosper T.
DASHER	P280	1988	Vosper T.
PUNCHER	P291	1988	Vosper T.
CHARGER	P292	1988	Vosper T.
RANGER	P293	1988	Vosper T.
TRUMPETER	P294	1988	Vosper T.

Displacement 43 tonnes **Dimensions** 20m x 6m x 1m **Speed** 20 knots **Armament** 1 x GPMG (Cyprus based vessels) **Complement** 5 (with accommodation for up to 12 under-graduates).

Notes
In service with RN University units (URNU) as training vessels. Commodore Britannia Royal Naval College has overall responsibility for the URNUs. Vessels are assigned to the following URNUs: ARCHER (Aberdeen); BITER (Manchester); BLAZER (Southampton); CHARGER (Liverpool); TRUMPETER (Bristol); EXAMPLE (Northumbria); EXPLOIT (Birmingham); EXPLORER (Yorkshire); EXPRESS (Wales); PUNCHER (London); RANGER (Sussex); RAIDER (Cambridge); SMITER (Glasgow); TRACKER (Oxford).
DASHER and PURSUER were transferred to Cyprus at the end of 2002 to form a new Cyprus Squadron to patrol off the Sovereign Base Areas. Based within RAF Akrotiri the boats are primarily employed in Force Protection of visiting ships and designated high value units.

HMS Scott

SURVEY SHIPS

Ship	Pennant Number	Completion Date	Builder
SCOTT	H 131	1997	Appledore

Displacement 13,300 tonnes **Dimensions** 131.5m x 21.5m x 9m **Speed** 17 knots
Complement 63

Notes

Designed to commercial standards SCOTT provides the RN with a deep bathymetric
capability off the continental shelf. Fitted with a modern multi-beam sonar suite she can
conduct mapping of the ocean floor worldwide. She carries a mixture of the latest UK and
US survey equipment. The sonar system is US supplied. She operates a three watch
system whereby the vessel is run by 42 of her ships company of 63 - with the remainder
on leave. Each crew member works 75 days in the ship before having 30 days off, allowing her to spend more than 300 days at sea in a year. These manpower reductions over
previous survey ships have been possible because of the extensive use of commercial
lean manning methods including unmanned machinery spaces, fixed fire fighting systems
and extensive machinery and safety surveillance technology.

HMS Echo

ECHO CLASS

Ship	Pennant Number	Completion Date	Builder
ECHO	H 87	2002	Appledore
ENTERPRISE	H 88	2003	Appledore

Displacement 3,470 tonnes **Dimensions** 90m x 16.8m x 5.5.m **Speed** 15 knots **Armament** 1 x 20mm **Complement** 46 (with accommodation for 81)

Notes

In June 2000, a £130 million order was placed with prime contractor Vosper Thornycroft to build and maintain, over a 25 year period, these two new Survey Vessels Hydrographic Oceanographic (SVHO). Both vessels were built by sub-contractor Appledore Shipbuilding Limited. They have a secondary role as mine countermeasures flag ships. The total Ship's Company is 72, with 48 personnel onboard at any one time working a cycle of 75 days on, 30 days off, allowing the ships to be operationally available for 330 days a year. Utilizing a diesel electric propulsion system, they have three main generators. They are the first RN ships to be fitted with Azimuth pod thrusters in place of the more normal shaft and propellor. Each ship carries a named survey launch, PATHFINDER (ECHO) and PIONEER (ENTERPRISE).

HMS Roebuck

COASTAL SURVEY VESSEL

Ship	Pennant Number	Completion Date	Builder
ROEBUCK	H130	1986	Brooke Marine

Displacement 1500 tonnes **Dimensions** 64m x 13m x 4m **Speed** 15 knots
Armament 1 x 20mm; Mk 44 Mini-guns **Complement** 51.

Notes

Able to operate for long periods away from shore support, this ship and the other vessels of the Hydrographic Fleet collect the data that is required to produce the Admiralty Charts and publications which are sold to mariners worldwide. Fitted with the latest fixing aids and sector scanning sonar. Emerged from a refit at Devonport in 2005 which will allow the ship to serve until 2014. Upgrades have included a new armament to complement the emerging frontline operational role for the survey squadron.

HMS Gleaner

INSHORE SURVEY VESSEL

Ship	Pennant Number	Completion Date	Builder
GLEANER	H86	1983	Emsworth

Displacement 22 tons **Dimensions** 14.8m x 4.7m x 1.3m **Speed** 14 knots
Complement 5.

Notes
Small inshore survey craft used for the collection of data from the shallowest inshore waters. Scheduled to decommission in 2007, she emerged, in 2008, from a Service Life Extention Programme, which will enable her to remain in service for a further 10 years. She will continue to conduct surveying operations around the UK coast.

HMS Endurance

ICE PATROL SHIP

Ship	Pennant Number	Completion Date	Builder
ENDURANCE	A171	1990	Ulstein-Hatlo

Displacement 5,129 tons **Dimensions** 91m x 17.9m x 6.5m **Speed** 14.9 knots
Armament Small arms **Aircraft** 2 Lynx **Complement** 116

Notes
Chartered for only 7 months in late 1991 to replace the older vessel of the same name. Originally M/V POLAR CIRCLE, renamed HMS POLAR CIRCLE (A176) and then purchased by MoD(N) and renamed again in October 1992 to current name. Historically spent 4-6 months each year in the South Atlantic supporting the British Antarctic Survey. In November 2007 she sailed for an 18 month deployment which will include two periods in the Antarctic, separated by a period of maritime security operations in the Atlantic Ocean. Crew rotation will enable the ship to remain on task for this extended period. The ship will remain in service until at least 2015.

Griffon 2000 TDX (M)

ROYAL MARINE CRAFT

4 GRIFFON 2000 TDX (M) LCAC

Pennants C21 - C24 **G.R.T.** 6.8 tons **Dimensions** 12m x 5m **Speed** 33 knots
Armament 1 x GPMG **Complement** 2

Notes
Ordered in April 1993, these four lightly armoured Landing Craft Air Cushion (LCAC)
are operated by 539 Assault Squadron. Used extensively during the Iraq War to patrol
the marshlands and waterways around Basra. They have the capacity to lift 12 fully
equipped troops or 2 x 1000kg pallets of stores and are capable of deployment in
C-130 Hercules transport aircraft. It is expected that the current fleet of hovercraft will
be replaced in the short term.

SPECIALIST CRAFT

In addition to the familiar Rigid Raiding Craft and Rigid Inflatable Boats the Royal
Marines have taken delivery of the Offshore Raiding Craft (ORC). It can be configured
to transport up to eight fully-equipped commandos at speeds of over 35 knots. It can
also be fitted with bullet-proof panels and weapon mountings to become a heavily-
armed fire support vessel. Other vessels available include Air transportable Fast
Insertion Craft (FIC) with a speed of 55 knots in addition to advanced wave piercing
designs. Swimmer Delivery Vehicles (SDV), in reality miniature submarines, which can
be deployed from dry deck shelters on larger submarines, are also a part of the UK
Special Forces inventory.

LCU Mk10

10 LCU Mk10

Pennants L1001 - L1010 **G.R.T.** 240 tons FL **Dimensions** 29.8m x 7.4m x 1.7m **Speed** 8.5 knots **Complement** 7.

Notes
Ro-Ro style landing craft designed to operate from the Albion class LPDs. Ordered in 1998 from Ailsa Troon. The first two were delivered in 1999. The remainder were built by BAE Systems at Govan. Capable of lifting one Main Battle Tank or four lighter vehicles. Capacity for 120 troops. Several older LCU Mk9s remain in service and saw service in Kuwait during the Iraq War.

23 LCVP Mk5

Pennants 9473, 9673-9692, 9707, 9708 **G.R.T.** 25 tons FL **Dimensions** 15m x 4m x 1.5m **Speed** 20 knots **Complement** 3.

Notes
First one ordered in 1995 from Vosper Thornycroft and handed over in 1996. A further four were delivered in December 1996 to operate from OCEAN, with two more for training at RM Poole ordered in 1998. A further 16 were ordered from Babcock in 2001. The Mk 5 can lift 8 tonnes of stores or a mix of 2 tonnes and 35 troops. These vessels have a greater range, lift and speed than the Mk 4s which they are gradually replacing.

SHIPS FOR THE FUTURE FLEET

FUTURE CARRIER PROGRAMME (CVF)

Contracts to build the aircraft carriers QUEEN ELIZABETH and PRINCE OF WALES, the largest warships to be designed and built in the UK, were signed by the MoD and industry on 3 July 2008.

The manufacturing contracts, worth in the region of £3 billion, were signed with a new UK maritime joint venture, formed by BAE Systems and VT Group, called BVT Surface Fleet, and the Aircraft Carrier Alliance onboard the aircraft carrier and Fleet Flagship ARK ROYAL at Portsmouth.

Hull sections will be built at Portsmouth, Govan and Barrow with final assembly to take place at Rosyth.

The carriers are expected to enter service in 2014 and 2016 respectively; once they enter service they are expected to remain in the fleet for at least thirty years (although previous announcements foresaw a service life approaching 50 years). ARK ROYAL and ILLUS-TRIOUS will decommission in 2012 and 2015 respectively.

With the present world financial situation there have been rumours about the cancellation of this project. However, throughout 2008 large contracts continued to be placed with industry for significant items of equipment and machinery and positive noises about the project continue to come out of the MoD.

SUSTAINED SURFACE COMBATANT CAPABILITY (S2C2) / FUTURE SURFACE COMBATANT (FSC)

The failed Future Surface Combatant study was replaced by S2C2 and broadened in scope to include replacement of MCM, Patrol and hydrographic ships, but now seems to have morphed back in the FSC programme. The current study appears to favour a range of three designs; a high capability ASW vessel (C1); a lower capability stabilisation vessel (C2) and an Ocean-Capable patrol vessel (C3). C1 and C2 are expected to be based on a common hull with a displacement of 6,000 tons and C3 is likely to be around 2,000 tons. Recognising the necessity to move forward with the C1 component of the project, a key decision was taken as part of the PR08 planning round. Rather than proceed with plans to procure the seventh and eighth Type 45 destroyers, resources are to be redirected towards accelerating the introduction of the C1 variant of FSC. This measure will bring forward the planned introduction into service of the first-of-class from 2021 to 2019.

Announcing this move in a parliamentary debate on 19 June 2008, Armed Forces minister Bob Ainsworth said it had been "a difficult decision", but added that FSC was being brought forward "to ensure our future naval capability and maintain the tempo of work for industry". He added: "That decision will result in a steady rhythm of building in our yards—from the six Type 45s, through the Future Carrier programme and into the [FSC] programme."

Under current plans, C1 is expected to achieve Initial Gate in mid-2009. A Main Gate decision to move into Demonstration and Manufacture is scheduled to follow in late 2011. Of course affordability figures prominently and FSC will be required to come in at a unit cost significantly below that of a Type 45, which means adopting proven equipments, avoiding over-specification and requirements change, and simplifying acceptance regimes.

MILITARY AFLOAT REACH AND SUSTAINABILITY (MARS)

The future re-equipment of the RFA rests with this programme in which it is envisioned 11 ships will be procured (Five fleet tankers - delivered 2011 to 2015; Three joint sea-based logistics vessels - 2016, 2017 and 2020; Two fleet solid-support ships - 2017 and 2020 and a single fleet tanker - 2021).
At the end of 2007 the MoD invited industry to express their interest in the project to build up to six fleet tankers. In May 2008 four companies had been shortlisted to submit proposals for the design and construction of the ships - Fincantieri (Italy); Hyundai (Republic of Korea); Navantia (Spain) and BAE Systems, teamed with BMT DSL and DSME (Republic of Korea). Initially none of the bidders were to build the ships in the UK, however, in November 2008 Fincatieri had teamed up with Northwestern Shiprepairers and Shipbuilders (NSL), formerly known as Cammell Laird. If selected, two of the tankers could, potentially, be built at Birkenhead.

TRIDENT REPLACEMENT PROGRAMME

The programme to maintain the UK's nuclear deterrent beyond the life of the current system, with the introduction into service of the first of a new class of submarines in 2024, is at an early stage. The programme is currently in a two-year initial concept phase for the new class of submarines. This requires a series of important and difficult decisions to be taken by September 2009 to keep the programme on track. The MoD has appointed a Senior Responsible Owner to co-ordinate these decisions and other work to inform future decisions and to allocate funding to the various elements of the programme.
The current predicted cost of procuring the new nuclear deterrent is between £15 billion and £20 billion (2006-7 prices), as outlined in the 2006 White Paper, "The future of the UK's nuclear deterrent." The operating costs for the deterrent once the new class of submarines comes into service are estimated to be similar to those of the current deterrent. A UK National Audit Office report published in November 2008 warned that the tight timetable set for ensuring the seamless transition from the present Vanguard class to the new submarines is challenging. The Vanguard class is likely to start leaving service from the early 2020s and the programme requires the future nuclear deterrent to be in service by 2024. The report warned that the MoD needs to establish now how far the service life of the Vanguard class can be safely extended.

THE ROYAL FLEET AUXILIARY

The Royal Fleet Auxiliary (RFA) is a civilian manned fleet, owned by the Ministry of Defence. Traditionally, its main task has been to replenish warships of the Royal Navy at sea with fuel, food, stores and ammunition to extend their operations away from base support. However, as the RN surface fleet has shrunk, the RFA has shrunk with it and a review has been conducted to determine the shape and role of the future RFA.

Contracts valued at around £250 million were placed by the MoD in 2008 with shipyards in the North West, North East and South West of England for the long-term maintenance of the RFA fleet.

Northwestern Shiprepairers and Shipbuilders (NSL) of Birkenhead and the A&P Group in Falmouth and Newcastle-upon-Tyne were named as the contractors to maintain the flotilla of 16 RFA tankers, stores and landing ships. The contractors will maintain 'clusters' of ships, providing the necessary refuelling and refit work for the RFA vessels throughout their service lives. Ships are grouped in clusters according to their duties and capabilities. A&P Group are charged with two clusters (Cluster 1: ARGUS and Cluster 2: CARDIGAN BAY, LYME BAY, LARGS BAY, MOUNTS BAY) in a contract worth around £53 million with the work to be shared between its bases in Falmouth and on the Tyne, while NSL is contracted for the maintenance of four clusters of ships (Cluster 3: BAYLEAF, ORANGE-LEAF, BLACK ROVER, GOLD ROVER; Cluster 4: DILIGENCE, WAVE KNIGHT, WAVE RULER; Cluster 5: FORT AUSTIN, FORT ROSALIE and Cluster 6: FORT GEORGE, FORT VICTORIA), with contracts totalling over £180 million. The new programme is expected to save over £330 million on the previous arrangements which saw individual contracts competed as and when they were required.

GOLD ROVER arrived on Merseyside on 11 August 2008 for a £8.5m refit, the first under the new programme, carried out by NSL. The ship was expected to return to the fleet towards the end of 2008.

The current RFA fleet comprises just 16 ships; 6 Fleet and Support tankers, 2 Dry Cargo Fleet Replenishment Ships, 2 "one stop" replenishment ships, providing both dry stores and fuel, 4 Landing Ships Dock, 1 Aviation Training Ship and 1 Forward Repair Ship. The future lies with an ambitious ship replacement programme, the Military Afloat Reach and Sustainability (MARS) programme which initially envisioned a fleet of eleven new ships to be delivered by 2021.

SHIPS OF THE ROYAL FLEET AUXILIARY
Pennant Numbers

Ship	Pennant Number	Ship	Pennant Number	Ship	Pennant Number
BAYLEAF	A109	FORT ROSALIE	A385	LARGS BAY	L3006
ORANGELEAF	A110	FORT AUSTIN	A386	LYME BAY	L3007
DILIGENCE	A132	FORT VICTORIA	A387	MOUNTS BAY	L3008
ARGUS	A135	FORT GEORGE	A388	CARDIGAN BAY	L3009
GOLD ROVER	A271	WAVE KNIGHT	A389		
BLACK ROVER	A273	WAVE RULER	A390		

KEEP UP TO DATE
THROUGHOUT THE YEAR

Warship World is published six times a year (Jan, Mar, May, Jul, Sep, Nov) and gives you all the information necessary to keep this book updated throughout the year. Now in full colour.

RFA Wave Knight

FLEET TANKERS

WAVE CLASS

Ship	Pennant Number	Completion Date	Builder
WAVE KNIGHT	A 389	2002	BAE SYSTEMS
WAVE RULER	A 390	2002	BAE SYSTEMS

Displacement 31,500 tons (Full Load) **Dimensions** 196 x 27 x 10m **Speed** 18 knots
Armament 2 x Vulcan Phalanx (fitted for but not with), 2 x 30mm **Aircraft** 1 Merlin
Complement 80 (plus 22 Fleet Air Arm)

Notes

These 31,500-tonne ships are diesel-electric powered, with three refueling rigs, and
aviation facilities to operate Merlin helicopters. They have a cargo capacity of 16,900
tonnes (Fuel) and 915 tonnes (Dry Stores). They have spent extended periods in the
Caribbean conducting successful counter-narcotics operations with their embarked
RN helicopter.

RFA Orangeleaf

LEAF CLASS

Ship	Pennant Number	Completion Date	Builder
BAYLEAF	A109	1982	Cammell Laird
ORANGELEAF	A110	1982	Cammell Laird

Displacement 37,747 tons **Dimensions** 170m x 26m x 12m **Speed** 14.5 knots **Complement** 60.

Notes

Both are single-hulled ex-merchant ships, originally acquired for employment mainly on freighting duties. Both have been modified to enable them to refuel warships at sea. BAYLEAF is now MoD(N) owned, with ORANGELEAF on long-term bareboat charter. In 2007 ORANGELEAF completed a Service Life Extension Programme (SLEP) refit which will enable her to serve until 2017. Both are commercial Stat32 class tankers. ORANGELEAF is scheduled to decommission in 2009 and BAYLEAF in 2010. The MoD also has also renewed the charter of the commercial tanker MAERSK RAPIER. She is a multi-tasked tanker which supplies fuel to the naval facilities in the UK and abroad. The MoD charters the vessel to commercial companies when it is not in use for their own requirements.

RFA Black Rover

ROVER CLASS

Ship	Pennant Number	Completion Date	Builder
GOLD ROVER	A271	1974	Swan Hunter
BLACK ROVER	A273	1974	Swan Hunter

Displacement 11,522 tons **Dimensions** 141m x 19m x 7m **Speed** 18 knots **Armament** 2 - 20mm guns **Complement** 49/54

Notes

Small Fleet Tankers designed to supply warships with fresh water, dry cargo and refrigerated provisions, as well as a range of fuels and lubricants. Helicopter deck, but no hangar. Have been employed in recent years mainly as support for HM Ships operating around the Falkland Islands and as the FOST station tanker. GREY ROVER decommissioned in 2006 and will be followed by GOLD ROVER in 2009 and BLACK ROVER in 2010.

RFA Fort Austin

STORES VESSELS

FORT CLASS I

Ship	Pennant Number	Completion Date	Builder
FORT ROSALIE	A385	1978	Scott Lithgow
FORT AUSTIN	A386	1979	Scott Lithgow

Displacement 23,384 tons **Dimensions** 183m x 24m x 9m **Speed** 20 knots **Complement** 201, (120 RFA, 36 MoD Civilians & 45 Fleet Air Arm).

Notes

Full hangar and maintenance facilities are provided and up to four Sea King or Lynx helicopters can be carried for both the transfer of stores and anti-submarine protection of a group of ships (note: these ships are not cleared to operate Merlin). Both ships can be armed with 4 - 20mm guns. FORT ROSALIE is to decommission in 2013 and FORT AUSTIN in 2014.

RFA Fort Victoria (departing Portsmouth for refit)

REPLENISHMENT SHIPS
FORT CLASS II

Ship	Pennant Number	Completion Date	Builder
FORT VICTORIA	A387	1992	Harland & Wolff
FORT GEORGE	A388	1993	Swan Hunter

Displacement 35,500 tons **Dimensions** 204m x 30m x 9m **Speed** 20 knots **Armament** 4 - 30mm guns, 2 x Phalanx CIWS, Sea Wolf Missile System (Fitted for but not with) **Complement** 100 (RFA), 24 MoD Civilians, 32 RN and up to 122 Fleet Air Arm.

Notes

"One stop" replenishment ships with the widest range of armaments, fuel and spares carried. Can operate up to 5 Sea King/Lynx or 3 Merlin Helicopters (more in a ferry role) with full maintenance facilities onboard. Medical facilities were upgraded with a 12 bed surgical capability. Both are to remain in service until 2019. Since May 2007 FORT VICTORIA had been at extended readiness at Portsmouth but left under tow on 21 October 2008 to refit at Birkenhead.

RFA Mounts Bay

LANDING SHIP DOCK (AUXILIARY) BAY CLASS

Ship	Pennant Number	Completion Date	Builder
LARGS BAY	L3006	2006	Swan Hunter
LYME BAY	L3007	2007	Swan Hunter
MOUNTS BAY	L3008	2006	BAe SYSTEMS
CARDIGAN BAY	L3009	2007	BAe SYSTEMS

Displacement 16,190 tonnes **Dimensions** 176.6m x 26.4m x 5.1m **Speed** 18 knots **Armament** Fitted to receive in emergency **Complement** 60

Notes
LYME BAY, the final ship of the class was towed from Swan Hunters in 2006 for completion by BAE Systems and was handed over to the RFA on 2 August 2007. The dock is capable of operating LCU 10s and they carry two LCVP Mk5s. They can offload at sea, over the horizon. In addition to their war fighting role they could be well suited to disaster relief and other humanitarian missions. LARGS BAY was fitted with a Temporary Aircraft Shelter (TAS) in October 2007.

The last of the LSLs, SIR BEDIVERE, decommissioned on 18 February 2008 and, like her sister SIR GALAHAD, will transfer to Brazil after a refit at Falmouth.

• STEVE WRIGHT

RFA Diligence

FORWARD REPAIR SHIP

Ship	Pennant Number	Completion Date	Builder
DILIGENCE	A132	1981	Oesundsvarvet

Displacement 10,595 tons **Dimensions** 120m x 12m x 3m **Speed** 15 knots **Armament** 2 - 20mm **Complement** RFA 40, RN Personnel - approx 100.

Notes

Formerly the M/V Stena Inspector purchased (£25m) for service in the South Atlantic. Her deep diving complex was removed and workshops added. When not employed on battle repair duties can serve as support vessel for MCMVs and submarines on deployment. A probable replacement will be required, the likely earliest date for such being 2014. DILIGENCE returned to the UK at the end of 2006 after five years away. At the end of 2007 she completed a refit at Northwestern Shiprepairers and Shipbuilders Limited (NSSL), based in Birkenhead, which will enable ther to remain in service for a further 10 years.

46

RFA Argus

AVIATION TRAINING SHIP

Ship	Pennant Number	Completion Date	Builder
ARGUS	A135	1981	Cantieri Navali Breda

Displacement 28,481 tons (full load) **Dimensions** 175m x 30m x 8m **Speed** 18 knots
Armament 4 - 30 mm, 2 - 20 mm **Complement** 254 (inc 137 Fleet Air Arm)
Aircraft 6 Sea King/Merlin, 12 Harriers can be carried in a "ferry role".

Notes
Formerly the M/V CONTENDER BEZANT taken up from trade during the Falklands crisis. Purchased in 1984 (£13 million) for conversion to an 'Aviation Training Ship'. A £50 million re-build was undertaken at Belfast from 1984-87. Undertook rapid conversion in October 1990 to a Primary Casualty Reception Ship for service in the Gulf. These facilities were upgraded and made permanent during 2001. Originally scheduled to decommission in 2008, this date has now been extended to 2020. A replacement for the Aviation Ship and PCRS role is currently under review. A new RFA PCRS is almost certain, but probably not in a dual role. If a new purpose-built/adapted ship is not acquired a likely scenario is that other RFAs with deck/hangar facilities will be used for aviation training (as is the case now when ARGUS is unavailable) or the task may be carried out by RN ships with flight decks.

47

MV Anvil Point

STRATEGIC SEALIFT
RO-RO VESSELS

Ship	Pennant Number	Completion Date	Builder
HURST POINT		2002	Flensburger
HARTLAND POINT		2002	Harland & Wolff
EDDYSTONE		2002	Flensburger
LONGSTONE		2003	Flensburger
ANVIL POINT		2003	Harland & Wolff
BEACHY HEAD		2003	Flensburger

Displacement 10,000 tonnes, 13,300 tonnes (FL) **Dimensions** 193m x 26m x 6.6m
Speed 18 knots **Complement** 38

Notes
Foreland Shipping Limited (formerly AWSR) built 6 ro-ro vessels at yards in the UK and Germany under a PFI deal which was signed with the MoD on 27 June 2002 and runs until 31 December 2024. While the current main focus is on transporting equipment to and from the Middle East/Gulf in support of military activities in Iraq and Afghanistan, the vessels also make regular voyages to the Falkland Islands and to Canada and Norway in support of training exercises. Two vessels not employed by the MoD, BEACHY HEAD and LONGSTONE, are on charter to Transfennica, a Finnish subsidiary of the Spliethoff Group. The six ships are all named after English lighthouses. The ships come under the operational umbrella of Defence Supply Chain Operation and Movements (DSCOM), part of the Defence Logistics Organisation.

HMS BULWARK

Cor Van Neikerken

HMS GLOUCESTER

Mark Bontemps

Daniel Ferro

HMS SCIMITAR

P294

HMS CHATHAM

Anthony Vella

Jim Patchett

RFA MOUNTS BAY

HMS EXETER

Steve Wright

D89

Nick Newns

HMS ARGYLL

F231

Mike Welsford

SERCO DENHOLM MARINE SERVICES

In December 2007 the MoD signed a £1 billion Private Finance Initiative (PFI) contract with Serco Denholm Marine Services Limited for the future provision of marine services (FPMS) over the next 15 years.

Serco manage, operate and maintain around 110 vessels used in both port and deep water operations. Over 30 new vessels will be introduced into service during the contract which covers the UK's major ports at Portsmouth, Devonport, and the Clyde. The majority of the new vessels will be constructed by the Netherlands based Damen Shipyards Group. Included are tugs, pilot boats and service craft.

The majority of marine services have been delivered by Serco Denholm under three Ports' Contracts since 1996, and by the Royal Maritime Auxiliary Service (RMAS). RMAS staff transfered entirely to Serco in April 2008. The RMAS, which was formed with Royal Assent in 1970, was disbanded at the end of March 2008.

Marine services embrace a wide range of waterborne and associated support activities, both in and out of port, at Portsmouth, Devonport and on the Clyde, as well as maintenance of UK and overseas moorings and navigational marks and support of a range of military operations and training.

In-port services include the provision of berthing and towage activities within the three naval bases; passenger transportation, including pilot transfers and the transportation of stores, including liquids and munitions. The recovery and disposal of waste from ships and spillage prevention and clean-up also fall within their tasking. There is also a requirement for substantial out-of-port operations. Diving training, minelaying exercises, torpedo recovery, boarding training and target towing duties are also undertaken.

The Briggs Group, has been sub-contracted to provide buoys and mooring support work. Shore based work to support the moorings and navigation buoys, relocated from Pembroke Dock to Burntisland on the Firth of Forth.

All vessels now have red funnels with the Serco Denholm house flag super-imposed. Hulls are now completely black, the white line having been removed as have, in most cases, the pennant numbers. All names are now prefixed with the letters 'SD' and all vessels fly the red ensign.

THE NEW BUILD FLEET

Information from Serco Denholm and the Dutch firm, Damen Shipyards, regarding the new build contracts for replacement vessels has been difficult to come by, and while many of the new vessels will be in service and seen around the ports during 2009/10 it is not possible to create full entries for the vessels until such information has been provided by the contractors.

There have been many rumours about the future of the remaining "legacy" RMAS fleet vessels. Some of the existing TUTTs, the 'Imp' class and SD ATLAS will be retained. It is thought that the best of the TUTT fleet will be assembled at, and operated from, Devonport, but I have been unable to confirm this, although it has been confirmed that some of the current fleet tugs are set for a service life extension programme. As details and dispersal of the new build vessels become more apparent, it will be easier to see which legacy vessels will remain and which will be disposed of.

The new tugs being built by Damen will be more powerful than those currently in use and have been designed to operate with the new generation of large RN vessels, the aircraft carriers, Type 45 destroyers and Astute class submarines.

Details of the Serco/Damen contracts are listed below, and where known proposed ship names and delivery dates are included.

The full contract covers:

DAMEN STAN TUG 1405 (1)

(SD TILLY)

A larger and more powerful workboat than the Pushy Cat 1204, this vessel was scheduled to be delivered by the end of 2008.

DAMEN ASD TUG 2009 (4)

(SD EILEEN, SD SUZANNE, SD CHRISTINA and SD DEBORAH)

To be delivered in 2010, these vessels have been developed from Damen's ASD 2411 these tugs will will be capable of harbour and coastal towing duties and are designed to handle smaller vessels, barges and submarine movements. This harbour and coastal tug, the vessel will have a bollard pull of 23.4 tons and maximum

• HANS ROSENKRANTZ   **SD Hercules**

speed of 11 knots. Equipped with winches fore and aft. In common with other tugs in the package, there will be facilities to accommodate passengers.

DAMEN STAN TUG 2608 (3)

(SD HERCULES, SD MARS and SD JUPITER)

The first was scheduled to be delivered in 2008, with the remaining pair in 2009. These are conventional twin screw tugs for coastal and port operations. Will have a comprehensive equipment fit enabling these vessels to conduct a wide variety of tasks. A double drum towing winch and deck crane will be fitted and will have a clear after deck the deployment and recovery of towed arrays. With the addition of an accommodation module can increase the number of personnel that can be carried from 12 to 30.

DAMEN ASD TUG 2509 (2)

(SD INDEPENDENT and SD INDULGENT)

Scheduled to be delivered in October and November of 2009. Two larger Azimuth Stern Drive tugs equipped with a bow thruster. Will be fitted with two double drum

59

towing winches along with underwater fendering, fire fighting equipment and facilities for passenger and stores transportation. May be used for harbour and coastal towing and the deployment and recovery of towed array.

DAMEN ATD TUG 2909 (4)

(SD RELIABLE; SD BOUNTIFUL; SD RESOURCEFUL and SD DEPENDABLE)

All to be delivered in 2010 these four vessels represent the largest tugs to be acquired under this contract. designated the Damen ATD Tug 2909. These vessels will be used to assist the new aircraft carriers and larger RN & RFA vessels due to enter service. The tugs will have a relatively shallow draft of 4.80m and incorporate extensive fendering above and below the waterline.

DAMEN PUSHY CAT 1204 (2)

(SD CATHERINE and SD EMILY)

See entry on page 67.

DAMEN MULTI CAT 2510 (2)

(SD NAVIGATOR and SD RAASAY)

To be delivered in 2009 - one will be configured for mooring and buoy handling while the other will be fitted for trials and be capable of supporting deployment and recovery of towed arrays, torpedo recovery and diving training.

DAMEN FAST CREW SUPPLIER 3307 (1)

(SD EVA)

To be delivered in 2009 this Axe-bowed crew transport vessel is likely to be used on the Clyde, as a replacement for SD ADAMANT, to transfer submarine crews and training personnel to and from vessels offshore in conditions of up to sea state 4. With a maximum speed of 22 knots, the vessel will be able to transport up to 34 passenger, all in individual seats.

WORLDWIDE SUPPORT SHIP 8316 (1)

(SD VICTORIA)

Being built by Damens Galatz Shipyard the ship is scheduled to be completed in mid-2010. Anticipated to be a direct replacement for the former cable layer and trials ship SD NEWTON. At 83 metres in length the ship will be capable of worldwide deployment and be able to conduct military training activities in addition to supporting military operations by the transportation of equipment and personnel. The design includes provision of classrooms, briefing and operations rooms, workshops, extensive storage areas, a helicopter winching deck, and provision to carry and operate Rigid Inflatable Boats.

Smaller vessels include 3 x Damen Stan Tender 1505 (SD CLYDE RACER, SD SOLENT RACER and SD TAMAR RACER) - Employed as Admiralty pilot launches, all delivered in 2008; 3 x Damen Stan Tender 1905 (SD CLYDE SPIRIT; SD SOLENT SPIRIT and SD TAMAR SPIRIT) - Employed as VIP and pilot launches all delivered in 2008.

The contract also includes construction and delivery of 1 x Damen Water Lighter Barge 3009 (SD WATERPRESS), 1 x Damen Diesel Lighter Barge 2909 (SD OILMAN) and 1 x Damen Liquid Mixed Lighter Barge 4315 (SD SEASPRAY).

In addition to the Damen-built vessels, Serco have ordered two 50.9m platform support vessels. Designed by Henderson International they are being built by ADYard, Abu Dhabi. These twin screw vessels, based on a small, shallow draft, anchor handler design, will incorporate a large clear after deck, winches and a deck crane.

The Briggs Group are supporting Serco by providing services for navigation buoys and mooring maintenance support and to this end Damen supplied the 61-metre Buoy Handling Vessel (Damen AHTS 6114) KINGDOM OF FIFE in 2008. Briggs are also believed to be operating SD ENGINEER (ex FORTH ENGINEER) at Devonport and SD INSPECTOR (ex-DMS EAGLE) at Portsmouth. A Multi Cat 2611 FORTH JOUSTER is also believed to be operated in support of the Briggs sub-contract.

SHIPS OF
SERCO DENHOLM MARINE SERVICES

Ship	Page	Ship	Page
CAPABLE	64	SD MEON	78
SD ADAMANT	77	SD MOORFOWL	83
SD ADEPT	64	SD MOORHEN	83
SD ATLAS	66	SD MYRTLE	68
SD BOUNTIFUL	60	SD NAVIGATOR	60
SD BOVISAND	72	SD NETLEY	73
SD BUSTLER	64	SD NEWHAVEN	73
SD CAREFUL	64	SD NEWTON	70
SD CATHERINE	67	SD NIMBLE	64
SD CAWSAND	72	SD NORTON	77
SD CHRISTINA	58	SD NUTBOURNE	73
SD CLYDE RACER	61	SD OBAN	74
SD CLYDE SPIRIT	61	SD OILMAN	61
SD COLONEL TEMPLER	71	SD OILPRESS	79
SD DEBORAH	58	SD OMAGH	74
SD DEPENDABLE	60	SD ORONSAY	74
SD DEXTEROUS	64	SD PADSTOW	75
SD EILEEN	58	SD PENRYN	77
SD EMILY	67	SD POWERFUL	64
SD ENGINEER	61	SD RAASAY	60
SD EVA	60	SD RELIABLE	60
SD FAITHFUL	64	SD RESOURCEFUL	60
SD FLORENCE	69	SD SALMAID	82
SD FORCEFUL	64	SD SALMOOR	82
SD FRANCES	69	SD SALUKI	65
SD GENEVIEVE	69	SD SEASPRAY	61
SD HELEN	69	SD SHEEPDOG	65
SD HERCULES	59	SD SOLENT RACER	61
SD HUSKY	65	SD SOLENT SPIRIT	61
SD IMPETUS	63	SD SPANIEL	65
SD IMPULSE	63	SD SPARROW	77
SD INDEPENDENT	59	SD STARLING	77
SD INDULGENT	59	SD SUZANNE	58
SD INSPECTOR	61	SD TAMAR RACER	61
SD JACKIE	77	SD TAMAR SPIRIT	61
SD JUPITER	59	SD TILLY	58
SD KITTY	68	SD TORMENTOR	81
SD KYLE OF LOCHALSH	84	SD TORNADO	81
SD LESLEY	68	SD VICTORIA	61
SD MARS	59	SD WARDEN	84
SD MELTON	78	SD WATERMAN	80
SD MENAI	78	SD WATERPRESS	61

SD Impulse

TUGS

IMPULSE CLASS

Ship	Completion Date	Builder
SD IMPULSE	1993	R. Dunston
SD IMPETUS	1993	R. Dunston

G.R.T. 400 tons approx **Dimensions** 33m x 10m x 4m **Speed** 12 knots
Complement 5.

Notes
Completed in 1993 specifically to serve as berthing tugs for the Trident Class submarines at Faslane. Likely to be retained in service.

SD Bustler

TWIN UNIT TRACTOR TUGS (TUTT's)

Ship	Completion Date	Builder
SD FORCEFUL	1985	R. Dunston
SD NIMBLE	1985	R. Dunston
SD POWERFUL	1985	R. Dunston
SD ADEPT	1980	R. Dunston
SD BUSTLER	1981	R. Dunston
CAPABLE	1981	R. Dunston
SD CAREFUL	1982	R. Dunston
SD FAITHFUL	1985	R. Dunston
SD DEXTEROUS	1986	R. Dunston

G.R.T. 375 tons **Dimensions** 39m x 10m x 4m **Speed** 12 knots **Complement** 9.

Notes

The principal harbour tugs in naval service. Some are to undergo a service life extension programme. CAPABLE continues to operate at Gibraltar but has not received an SD prefix. Reluctantly Serco had intended to charter in tugs as required but the MoD insisted that she be retained primarily for the movement of nuclear-powered submarines. Serco agreed but they have left this department to continue as it was.

SD Sheepdog

DOG CLASS

Ship	Completion Date	Builder
SD HUSKY	1969	Appledore
SD SALUKI	1969	Appledore
SD SPANIEL	1967	Appledore
SD SHEEPDOG	1969	Appledore

G.R.T. 152 tons **Dimensions** 29m x 8m x 4m **Speed** 12 knots **Complement** 5.

Notes
General harbour tugs – all completed between 1965 and 1969. SALUKI operates at Devonport, SHEEPDOG was scheduled to be withdrawn in 2005 but remains in service at Portsmouth. SPANIEL and HUSKY operate on the Clyde.

SD Atlas

UZMAR CLASS

Ship	Completion Date	Builder
SD ATLAS	1999	Uzmar, Turkey

G.R.T. 88 tons **Dimensions** 21.3m x 7.6m x 3.3m **Speed** 12.5 knots **Complement** 8

Notes

The former Turkish built tug MT YENIKALE was renamed MT ATLAS and bareboat chartered by Serco Denholm in 2005 for service at Portsmouth. The name Atlas was chosen as it was the name of one of the early Pilot Class of tugs built in Chatham Dockyard in 1909. The vessel is designed for Coastal and Harbour Towage. She has a bollard pull of 33 tonnes.

SD Emily

PUSHY CAT 1204

Ship	Completion Date	Builder
SD CATHERINE	2008	Damen Shipyards, NL
SD EMILY	2008	Damen Shipyards, NL

G.R.T. 30 tons **Dimensions** 12m x 3.84m x 1.75m **Speed** 8.5 knots **Complement** 3

Notes
First of the new build Damen tugs, acquired as part of the Marine Services contract, to enter service. SD CATHERINE allocated to Portsmouth. SD EMILY the Clyde.

SD Myrtle

TRITON CLASS

Ship	Completion Date	Builder
SD KITTY	1972	R. Dunston
SD LESLEY	1973	R. Dunston
SD MYRTLE	1973	R. Dunston

G.R.T. 89 tons **Speed** 8 knots **Complement** 4.

Notes

Known as Water Tractors these craft are used for basin moves and towage of light barges. KITTY was proposed to be withdrawn from operations in 2003 but remains in service at Portsmouth. LESLEY and MYRTLE operate at Devonport.

SD Florence

FELICITY CLASS

Ship	Completion Date	Builder
SD FLORENCE	1980	R. Dunston
SD FRANCES	1980	R. Dunston
SD GENEVIEVE	1980	R. Dunston
SD HELEN	1974	R. Dunston

G.R.T. 80 tons **Speed** 10 knots **Complement** 4.

Notes
Water Tractors used for the movement of small barges and equipment. Two sister vessels (GEORGINA and GWENDOLINE) sold to Serco Denholm in 1996 for service in H M Naval bases. FLORENCE and FRANCES operate at Devonport, GENEVIEVE and HELEN at Portsmouth.

SD Newton

RESEARCH VESSEL

Ship	Completion Date	Builder
SD NEWTON	1976	Scotts

G.R.T. 2,779 tons **Dimensions** 99m x 16m x 6m **Speed** 15 knots **Complement** 27

Notes

Primarily used in the support of military training exercises. Some limited support provided for various trials. Completed major refit in 2001 to extend life. Is frequently seen with Royal Marine small craft embarked and is used as a training platform. Likely to be replaced in 2010 by the new Worldwide Support Ship, SD VICTORIA.

SD Colonel Templer

REASEARCH VESSEL

Ship	Completion Date	Builder
SD COLONEL TEMPLER	1966	Hall Russell

Displacement 1,300 tons **Dimensions** 56m x 11m x 5.6 m **Speed** 12 knots
Complement 14

Notes

Built as a stern trawler but converted in 1980 for use by the Defence Evaluation and
Research Agency as an acoustic research vessel. A major rebuild was completed after
a serious fire gutted the ship in 1990. 12 scientists can be carried. From Nov 2000 operated on the Clyde. Used in support of trials and converted in 2001 to support RN diving
training. The forward 'A' frame has been painted red with a black top.

SD Cawsand

TENDERS
STORM CLASS

Ship	Completion Date	Builder
SD BOVISAND	1997	FBM (Cowes)
SD CAWSAND	1997	FBM (Cowes)

G.R.T 225 tonnes **Dimensions** 23m x 11m x 2m **Speed** 15 knots **Complement** 5

Notes

These craft are used in support of Flag Officer Sea Training (FOST) at Plymouth to transfer staff quickly and comfortably to and from Warships and Auxiliaries within and beyond the Plymouth breakwater in open sea conditions. These are the first vessels of a small waterplane area twin hull (SWATH) design to be ordered by the Ministry of Defence and cost £6.5 million each. Speed restrictions implemented due to wash problems generated by these vessels.

SD Nutbourne

NEWHAVEN CLASS

Ship	Completion Date	Builder
SD NEWHAVEN	2000	Aluminium SB
SD NUTBOURNE	2000	Aluminium SB
SD NETLEY	2001	Aluminium SB

Tonnage 77 tonnes (45 grt) **Dimensions** 18.3m x 6.8m x 1.88m **Speed** 10 knots **Complement** 3 Crew (60 passengers).

Notes
MCA Class IV Passenger Vessels based at Portsmouth as replacements for Fleet tenders. Employed on general passenger duties within the port area.

SD Omagh

OBAN CLASS

Ship	Completion Date	Builder
SD OBAN	2000	McTay
SD ORONSAY	2000	McTay
SD OMAGH	2000	McTay

Tonnage 199 tons **Dimensions** 27.7m x 7.30m x 3.75m **Speed** 10 knots **Complement** 5 Crew (60 passengers).

Notes
MCA Class IIA Passenger Vessels which replaced Fleet tenders in 2001. OBAN was transferred to Devonport in 2003 for use in supporting passenger transfers and is occasionally used in support of FOST staff. ORONSAY and OMAGH employed on general passenger duties on the Clyde and are additionally classified as Cargo Ship VIII(A).

SD Padstow

PADSTOW CLASS

Ship	Completion Date	Builder
SD PADSTOW	2000	Aluminium SB

Tonnage 77 tonnes (45 grt) **Dimensions** 18.3m x 6.8m x 1.88m **Speed** 10 knots **Complement** 3 Crew (60 passengers).

Notes
MCA Class IV, VI and VIA Passenger Vessel based at Plymouth. Used on general passenger ferrying duties and in support of FOST staff.

• MIKE PALMER

SD Penryn

• MIKE PALMER

SD Norton

SD Adamant

PERSONNEL FERRY

Ship	Completion Date	Builder
SD ADAMANT	1992	FBM (Cowes)

G.R.T 170 tonnes **Dimensions** 30m x 8m x 1m **Speed** 22 knots **Complement** 5

Notes

Twin catamaran hulls based on the commercial Red Jet design (as used by Red Funnel Ferry Co). First water jet propulsion vessel owned by MoD(N). In service as a Clyde personnel ferry.

A former civilian vessel FIONAN OF SKILLIG, operated by MoD (as D12) in support of FOST since 1996, has received a full black and buff livery and has been renamed SD PENRYN.

The single FBM catamaran, 8837, operated at Portsmouth, has now been renamed SD NORTON while two snub-nosed harbour launches have been named SD SPARROW and SD STARLING.

An 11 metre harbour launch employed at Devonport on pollution control duties has been named SD JACKIE.

SD Melton

FLEET TENDERS

Ship	Completion Date	Builder
SD MELTON	1981	Richard Dunston
SD MENAI	1981	Richard Dunston
SD MEON	1982	Richard Dunston

G.R.T. 78 tons **Dimensions** 24m x 6m x 3m **Speed** 10.5 knots **Complement** 4/5.

Notes

The last three survivors of a once numerous class of vessels used as Training Tenders, Passenger Ferries, or Cargo Vessels. MENAI and MEON are operated at Falmouth. MELTON is operated at Kyle. Remain in service pending a vessel replacement programme.

SD Oilpress

COASTAL OILER

Ship	Completion Date	Builder
SD OILPRESS	1969	Appledore Shipbuilders

G.R.T. 362 tons **Dimensions** 41m x 9m x 3m **Speed** 11 knots **Complement** 5.

Notes
Employed as Harbour and Coastal Oiler. Operated on the Clyde.

SD Waterman

WATER CARRIER

Ship	Completion Date	Builder
SD WATERMAN	1978	R. Dunston

G.R.T. 263 tons **Dimensions** 40m x 8m x 2m **Speed** 11 knots **Complement** 5.

Notes
Capable of coastal passages, but normally supplies either demineralised or fresh water to the Fleet within port limits.

SD Tormentor

TORPEDO RECOVERY VESSELS (TRV)
TORNADO CLASS

Ship	Completion Date	Builder
SD TORNADO	1979	Hall Russell
SD TORMENTOR	1980	Hall Russell

G.R.T. 560 tons **Dimensions** 47m x 8m x 3m **Speed** 14 knots **Complement** 13.

Notes
Both vessels have had suitable rails fitted to enable them to operate as exercise minelayers. Converted in 2002 to support RN diving training (in lieu of Fleet Tenders) in addition to their other roles. Both operate on the Clyde.

SD Salmoor

MOORING & SALVAGE VESSELS
SAL CLASS

Ship	Completion Date	Builder
SD SALMOOR	1985	Hall Russell
SD SALMAID	1986	Hall Russell

Displacement 2,200 tonnes **Dimensions** 77m x 15m x 4m **Speed** 15 knots **Complement** 19

Notes
Multi-purpose vessels designed to lay and maintain targets, navigation marks and moorings. SALMOOR is based at Greenock and SALMAID at Devonport. Both vessels can be deployed in support of submarine and submarine rescue operations.

SD Moorfowl

MOOR CLASS

Ship	Completion Date	Builder
SD MOORHEN	1989	McTay Marine
SD MOORFOWL	1989	McTay Marine

Displacement 518 tons **Dimensions** 32m x 11m x 2m **Speed** 8 knots **Complement** 10

Notes
Powered mooring lighters for use within sheltered coastal waters. Both operated in support of mooring maintenance. MOORHEN based at Portsmouth and MOORFOWL at Devonport. Both vessels also undertake coastal work.

SD Warden

TRIALS VESSEL

Ship	Completion Date	Builder
SD WARDEN	1989	Richards

Displacement 626 tons **Dimensions** 48m x 10m x 4m **Speed** 15 knots **Complement** 11.

Notes

Built as a Range Maintenance Vessel but now based at Kyle of Lochalsh and operated in support of BUTEC. Her earlier gantry has been removed and bridge structure extended aft. Also operates as a Remotely Operated Vehicle (ROV) platform. A replacement ROV has been installed and set to work to replace the older system.

There are two further trials craft on long term charter to help with the various tasks at the Kyle of Lochalsh. One is the SARA MAATJE VI on charter from Van Stee of Holland. The second is the twin screw tug MSC LENIE which has now been purchased from Maritime Craft Services (Clyde) Ltd by Serco Denholm. The 24.35m tug, built in 1997 by Abel in Bristol, is powered by Caterpillar main engines producing a total of 2,200bhp for a bollard pull of 26 tons. The vessel has been renamed SD KYLE OF LOCHALSH.

Smit Yare

AIRCREW TRAINING VESSELS

Ship	Comp Date	Builder	Base Port
SMIT DEE	2003	BES Rosyth	Bukie
SMIT DART	2003	BES Rosyth	Plymouth
SMIT DON	2003	BES Rosyth	Blyth
SMIT YARE	2003	FBMA Cebu	Great Yarmouth
SMIT TOWY	2003	FBMA Cebu	Pembroke Dock
SMIT SPEY	2003	FBMA Cebu	Plymouth

G.R.T. 95.86 GRT **Dimensions** 27.6m x 6.6m x 1.5m **Speed** 21 knots **Complement** 6

Notes
The vessels were designed by FBM Babcock Marine and built in their shipyards in Scotland and the Philippines. Operated by SMIT International (Scotland) on behalf of the MoD for training military aircrew in marine survival techniques, helicopter winching drills and general marine support tasks. The design includes an aft docking well for a RIB or for torpedo recovery, a full width stern training platform and clear deck areas for helicopter winching drills. SMIT DART completed as a passenger vessel with larger superstructure. Two similar second-hand vessels, SMIT TAMAR and SMIT CYMRYAN are also employed in the same role.

RANGE SAFETY VESSELS

Ship	Comp Date	Builder
SMIT STOUR	2003	Maritime Partners Norway
SMIT ROTHER	2003	Maritime Partners Norway
SMIT ROMNEY	2003	Maritime Partners Norway
SMIT CERNE	2003	Maritime Partners Norway
SMIT FROME	2003	Maritime Partners Norway
SMIT MERRION	2003	Maritime Partners Norway
SMIT PENALLY	2003	Maritime Partners Norway
SMIT WAY	2003	Maritime Partners Norway
SMIT NEYLAND	2003	Maritime Partners Norway

G.R.T. 7.0 GRT **Dimensions** 12.3m x 2.83m x 0.89m **Speed** 35 knots **Complement** 2

Notes
A class of 12 metre Fast Patrol Craft which operate on Range Safety Duties at Dover, Portland and Pembroke. Have replaced the former RCT Sir and Honours class launches in this role.

RCTV Audemer

RAMPED CRAFT LOGISTIC

Vessel	Pennant Number	Completion Date	Builder
ARROMANCHES	L105	1987	James & Stone
ANDALSNES	L107	1984	James & Stone
AKYAB	L109	1984	James & Stone
AACHEN	L110	1986	James & Stone
AREZZO	L111	1986	James & Stone
AUDEMER	L113	1987	James & Stone

Displacement 165 tons **Dimensions** 33m x 8m x 1.5m **Speed** 9 knots
Complement 6.

Notes
Operated by the Army's 17 Port and Maritime Regiment, Royal Logistic Corps, these all purpose landing craft are capable of carrying up to 96 tons. They are self sustaining for around five days or a thousand nautical miles before requiring replenishment either at sea or in a haven. In service in coastal waters around Cyprus (ANDALSNES and AKYAB) and UK. ARROMANCHES was formerly AGHEILA (re-named 1994 when original vessel was sold). Several vessels sport a green and black camouflage scheme.

AIRCRAFT OF THE FLEET AIR ARM

LEE HOWARD

BAE Systems HARRIER

Variants GR9, GR9A, T12.
Role Short take off, vertical landing (STOVL) strike, ground-attack and reconnaissance aircraft. T12 is two-seat trainer.
Engine 1 x Rolls Royce Pegasus 107 turbofan rated at 23,800lb thrust.
Span 30' 4"   **Length** 47' 1"   **Height** 11' 7"   **Max weight** 31,000lb.
Max speed 575 knots at low level.   **Crew** 1 pilot.
Avionics Hughes Angle Rate Bombing System (ARBS); thermal and infra-red imaging sensors; Zeus defensive aids suite including radar warning, ECM & chaff & flare dispensers; Night Vision Goggle (NVG) compatible cockpit.
Armament Up to 13,000lb of weapons on nine hard points. Inner wing stations can carry up to 2,000lb, outer wing stations intended only for Sidewinder missiles. Weapons include AGM 65 TV and IR guided air to surface missiles (ASM); Brimstone anti-armour ASM; Paveway II & III Laser Guided Bombs (LGB); CRV 7 rocket pods and up to 4 Sidewinder infra-red guided Air to Air Missiles (AAM). Inner wing stations carry 100 or 190 gallon drop tanks. A reconnaissance pod can be carried on the fuselage centre station.
Squadron Service 800 and 801 Squadrons operate as a single Naval Strike Wing within Joint Force Harrier.

Notes Shortage of pilots and extended operations in Afghanistan have continued to force the two small squadrons to operate as a single Wing within Joint Force Harrier. Embarkations in the carriers have been minimal but the deployment of Tornadoes to Afghanistan in 2009 should allow more time at sea in the operational carrier. Harriers are the only British fast-jets capable of operation from the future carriers when they are commissioned; present plans are for them to be replaced by the F-35B Lightning II Joint Strike Fighter from 2018. Harriers are shore-based at RAF Cottesmore.

AgustaWestland MERLIN

Variants HM1
Role Anti-submarine and Maritime patrol
Engine 3 x Rolls-Royce Turbomeca RTM322 turboshafts each developing 2,100 shp
Length 74' 10" **Width** 14' 10" **Height** 21' 10" **Main Rotor Diameter** 61'
Max Weight 32,120 lbs
Max Speed 167 kts   **Range** 625 nm
Crew 3 (Pilot, Observer and Aircrewman)
Avionics Blue Kestrel 360 degree search radar, Orange Reaper ESM, passive and active sonar systems and AQS903 digital processor.
Armament 4 lightweight torpedoes or depth charges.
Squadron Service 700M (OEU), 814, 820, 824, 829 Squadrons

Notes Merlin is a specialised anti-submarine helicopter with a limited surface search capability. Installation of the L-3 Wescam MX-15 electro-optical/infrared sensor has improved the latter capability as it is fitted, gradually, to the force but the type's usefulness is limited by the inability to carry an air-to-surface missile and the lack of a modern data link such as Link 16. 824 is the training unit and 829 is the parent unit for single aircraft flights deployed to Type 23 frigates. The other units deploy aircraft to make up TAGs in carriers and RFAs. All Merlin Squadrons are shore-based at RNAS Culdrose.

AgustaWestland SEA KING

The veteran Sea King continues in RN service after 40 years in a number of roles. The following details are common to all.

Engines 2 x 1600shp Rolls Royce Gnome H 1400 – 1 free power turbines.
Rotor Diameter 62' 0" **Length** 54' 9" **Height** 17' 2" **Max Weight** 21,400lb
Max Speed 125 knots.

NICK NEWNS

HAR 5 / 6

Roles Utility; COD (Carrier Onboard Delivery); SAR.
Crew 2 pilots, 1 observer and 1 aircrewman.
Avionics Sea Searcher radar; Orange Crop passive ESM equipment.
Armament A 7.62mm machine gun can be mounted in the doorway.
Squadron Service 771 Squadron
Notes 771 provides Sea King type-training and SAR coverage in the South West from RNAS Culdrose. Frequently embarked for utility duties.

ASaC 7

Role Airborne Surveilance and Control. **Crew:** 1 pilot and 2 observers.
Avionics Upgraded Thales Searchwater radar, Orange Crop passive ESM, Enhanced Communications System, Joint Tactical Information Distribution System (Link 16)
Squadron Service 849, 854, 857 Squadrons.

Notes Combining a modern radar system in airframes that are 40 years old, ASaC 7s are able to detect airborne, land and sea surface targets and to command and control allied forces making them invaluable assets in both littoral and open-ocean operations. The MOD hopes to keep the type in service until 2022 for operation from the 2 future carriers ordered in 2008. A Project to evaluate replacement options for the Sea King in this role has run for more than 10 years but has not resulted in any order for hardware. Squadrons are based at RNAS Culdrose when not embarked as part of a TAG.

HC 4, Mk6 (CR)

Role Commando assault and utility transport.
Crew 1 or 2 pilots and 1 aircrewman. **Armament** Door mounted 7.62mm machine gun.
Squadron Service 845, 846 and 848 Squadrons.
Notes The HC 4 is capable of carrying troops internally and underslung loads of up to 6,000lb, these 3 Squadrons are based at RNAS Yeovilton and form the RN element of the Joint Helicopter Command. The HC 4 can be fitted with armour over sensitive areas and a sophisticated defensive aids suite. Mk 6 airframes are used for training in the UK and do not deploy. RN Commando helicopters have operated extensively in Iraq and, from 2008, in Afghanistan. The HC 4 is expected to remain in service until 2022 despite the strain imposed by the tempo of operations in the foreseeable future. There is an urgent need to identify a replacement if the capability is to be retained.

Lynx HMA 8

Agusta-Westland LYNX

Variants HAS 3, HMA 8, AH 7.

Roles Surface search and attack; anti-submarine attack; SAR; troop carrying.

Engines 2 x 900hp Rolls Royce GEM BS 360-07-26 free shaft turbines.

Rotor diameter 42' 0" **Length** 39' 1" **Height** 11' 0" **Max Weight** 9,500lb.

Max Speed 150 knots. **Crew** 1 pilot and 1 observer.

Avionics SEA SPRAY radar. Orange Crop passive ESM equipment. Sea Owl Passive Infrared Device (Mk 8).

Armament External pylons carry up to 4 - SEA SKUA air to surface missiles or 2 x STINGRAY torpedoes, depth charges and markers. 1 door mounted M3M 0.5" machine gun. Standard configuration for board and search operations now 1 x door mounted M3M, 1 x pylon mounted Sea Skua and rope for "rapid-roping" deployment of troops.

Squadron Service 702, 815 and 847 Squadrons.

Notes 702 is the type training unit and 815 the parent squadron for Flights detached to Type 42 destroyers and RFAs. 847 is a light strike and reconnaissance unit which operates alongside the 3 commando Sea King squadrons with the AH 7 military version recognised by its skid undercarriage. All are shore-based at RNAS Yeovilton. With its greater agility, smaller size and better range of weapons and sensors, the Lynx is a more valuable anti-surface vessel unit than the Merlin which was originally intended to replace it. It is the preferred option for the various 'board and search' operations carried out by the RN. 30 new helicopters based on a 'Super Lynx' design with options for 5 more, have been ordered and tentatively named the 'Wildcat II' for service from 2015. The RN has not stated from which ships they are intended to operate.

TAILORED AIR GROUPS

ILLUSTRIOUS, ARK ROYAL and OCEAN no longer have dedicated air groups but embark Tailored Air Groups (TAG) made up from different aircraft types from three different forces for specific missions. In the first two ships, 3 separate aircraft types can be embarked concurrently, in small numbers, selected from Harrier, Merlin, Sea King, Chinook and Apache squadrons. The Sea Kings are usually ASaC 7s but HC 4 and HAR 5 also embark. OCEAN cannot support fixed-wing aircraft operationally but they can land, refuel and launch from her deck. TAGs embark with appropriate force commanders responsible to PJHQ Northwood for the tactical employment of their aircraft and their own Naval or Joint Force HQ for their operational readiness. This concept has been evolved by the MOD for use in the RN's new carriers when they become operational. It is unique to the UK and has already proved significantly less effective in terms of operational capability than the dedicated air groups used previously by the RN. With so many air assets deployed ashore in Iraq and Afghanistan on a long-term basis the Fleet is finding the maintenance of a credible aviation capability to be a problem at a time when personnel skills of all types should be improving to meet the challenge of operating the new carriers. Apache and Chinook helicopters might be seen on deck as part of a TAG. Their particulars are:

● LEE HOWARD

AgustaWestland APACHE

Variants AH 1
Role Attack and reconnaissance helicopter.
Engines 2 x Rolls Royce/Turbomeca RTM 322 turboshafts.
Rotor Diameter 17' 2" **Length** 58' 3" **Height** 15' 3" **Max Weight** 15,075lb.
Max Speed 150 knots **Crew:** 2 pilots
Avionics Helicopter Integrated Defensive Aids Suite (HIDAS); Longbow radar, optical and infra-red target acquisition sensors.
Armament Up to 16 AGM 114 Hellfire anti-tank guided weapons; up to 4 Sidewinder air-to-air missiles; M230 30mm cannon with 1,160 rounds (chain gun); up to 76 CRV 7 unguided rockets.

Operator Operated by the Army Air Corps as part of the Joint Helicopter Force.

Notes Apaches are cleared for embarked operations but with the number deployed in support of land operations the opportunities for them to exercise in the amphibious role are limited.

• NICK NEWNS

Boeing CHINOOK

Variants HC 2
Role Battlefield transport helicopter.
Engines 2 x 3,750 shp Avco Lycoming T55-L-712 turboshafts.
Rotor Diameter 60' 0" **Length** 98' 9" **Height** 18' 8" **Max Weight** 50,000lb
Max Speed 160 knots **Crew** 2 pilots, 1 aircrewman.
Avionics Infra-red jammer; chaff & flare dispenser, missile warning system.
Armament Up to 2 x M 134 miniguns and 1 x M 60 machine gun.
Operator Operated by the RAF as part of the Joint Helicopter Force.
Notes RAF Chinook squadrons form part of the Joint Helicopter Force with the RN commando squadrons. 18 Squadron aircraft embarked in ARK ROYAL during Operation Telic in 2003 and are frequently used to provide heavy lift during amphibious expeditionary operations. They are too large to strike down into the hangars in OCEAN, ILLUSTRIOUS and ARK ROYAL and have to have their rotor blades manually removed for parking on deck as they lack a conventional blade fold mechanism. As with the Sea King, there seems to be little urgency to replace or augment the Chinook in the heavy lift role.

GALILEO AVIONICA

FLEET TARGET GROUP

792 Squadron operates Mirach 100/5 unmanned air vehicles (UAV) to test the Sea Dart missile systems fitted to Type 42 destroyers and the Sidewinder missiles carried by Harriers and RAF Tornadoes. The UAVs can be launched from the flight deck of a destroyer and Fort or Rover class RFAs and can be controlled by an operator in the ship or ashore. Once the UAV has completed its mission, it parachutes down into the sea if it has not been destroyed, to be recovered by helicopter and used again after refurbishment.

OTHER AIRCRAFT TYPES IN ROYAL NAVY SERVICE DURING 2009

BAE Systems HAWK

Engine 1 x Adour Mk 151 5200 lbs thrust.
Crew 1 or 2 Pilots (both service and civilian)
Notes Used by Fleet Requirements and Aircraft Direction Unit (FRADU) at Culdrose to provide support for training of RN ships, RN Flying Standards Flight and as airborne targets for the Aircraft Direction School. The aircraft are operated by Babcock.

BAE Systems JETSTREAM T2

Engines 2 x 940hp Turbomeca Astazou 16D turboprops. (T3 Garrett turboprops).
Crew 1 or 2 pilots, 2 student observers plus 3 other seats.
Notes Used by 750 Squadron at RNAS Culdrose to train Fleet Air Arm Observers. Due to be replaced by Beech King Air training aircraft, as part of the 'Ascent' Training Scheme adopted by the MOD, in the near future. The Jetstreams operated at Yeovilton were withdrawn in 2008.

Eurocopter AS365N DAUPHIN 2

Engines 2 x Turbomeca Arriel 1C1.
Crew 1 or 2 pilots.
Notes Operated by British International from Plymouth City Airport under MoD COMR (Civil Owned Military Registered) contract. Used to transfer Sea Training staff from shore and between ships operating in the Plymouth sea training areas during work-ups. Aircraft are also used for Guided Weapons System Calibration and Naval Gunfire Support.

GROB G115 D-2

Used for the flying grading of new entry aircrew and other light, fixed-wing tasks. They are civilian manned but operated on behalf of 727 squadron at RNAS Yeovilton.

Royal Navy Historic Flight

The Flight is based at RNAS Yeovilton where aircraft are maintained by civilians but flown by volunteer RN pilots. In 2009 the Flight comprises Swordfish I W5856, Swordfish II LS 326, Sea Fury FB 11 VR 930, Sea Hawk WV 908 and Chipmunk T10 WK 608, not all of which are serviceable at any one time. Swordfish III NF 389 is undergoing long-term restoration at BAE Systems' Brough factory and a Sea Fury T 20 VX 281/G-RNHF is due to join the Flight.

• LEE HOWARD   **Royal Navy Historic Flight Sea Fury FB.11 (VR930)**

• LEE HOWARD   **Royal Navy Historic Flight Swordfish I (W5856)**

Sea Launched Missiles

Trident II D5

The American built Lockheed Martin Trident 2 (D5) submarine launched strategic missiles are Britain's only nuclear weapons and form the UK contribution to the NATO strategic deterrent. 16 missiles, each capable of carrying up to 6 UK manufactured thermonuclear warheads (but currently limited to 4 under current government policy), are aboard each of the Vanguard class SSBNs. Trident has a maximum range of 12,000 km and is powered by a three stage rocket motor. Launch weight is 60 tonnes, overall length and width are 13.4 metres and 2.1 metres respectively.

Tomahawk (BGM-109)

This is a land attack cruise missile with a range of 1600 km and can be launched from a variety of platforms including surface ships and submarines. Some 65 of the latter version were purchased from America to arm Trafalgar class SSNs with the first being delivered to the Royal Navy for trials during 1998. Tomahawk is fired in a disposal container from the submarine's conventional torpedo tubes and is then accelerated to its subsonic cruising speed by a booster rocket motor before a lightweight F-107 turbojet takes over for the cruise. Its extremely accurate guidance system means that small targets can be hit with precision at maximum range, as was dramatically illustrated in the Gulf War and Afghanistan. Total weight of the submarine version, including its launch capsule is 1816 kg, it carries a 450 kg warhead, length is 6.4 metres and wingspan (fully extended) 2.54 m. Fitted in T class submarines.

Harpoon

The Harpoon is a sophisticated anti-ship missile using a combination of inertial guidance and active radar homing to attack targets out to a range of 130 km, cruising at Mach 0.9 and carrying a 227 kg warhead. Fitted to the Batch II Type 22 and Type 23 frigates. It is powered by a lightweight turbojet but is accelerated at launch by a booster rocket. The RN also deploys the UGM-84 submarine launched version aboard its Swiftsure and Trafalgar class SSNs.

Aster 15/30

Principal Anti-Air Missile System for Type 45 The missile that will arm the Royal Navy's new Type 45 Destroyers has proved it'argets out to a Two versions of the Aster missile will equip the Type 45 Destroyer, the shorter range Aster 15 and the longer range Aster 30. The missiles form the weapon component of the Principal Anti Air Missile System (PAAMS). Housed in a 48 cell Sylver Vertical Launch system, the missile mix can be loaded to match the ship s requirement. Aster 15 has a range of 30 km while Aster 30 can achieve 100 km. The prime external difference between the two is the size of the booster rocket attached to the bottom of the missile.

Sea Dart

A medium range area defence anti aircraft missile powered by a ramjet and solid fuel booster rocket. Maximum effective range is in the order of 80 km and the missile accelerates to a speed of Mach 3.5. It forms the main armament of the Type 42 destroyers. Missile weight 550 kg, length 4.4 m, wingspan 0.91 m.

Sea Wolf

Short range rapid reaction anti-missile missile and anti-aircraft weapon. The complete weapon system, including radars and fire control computers, is entirely automatic in operation. Type 22 frigates carry two sextuple Sea Wolf launchers but the subsequent Type 23 frigates carry 32 Vertical Launch Seawolf (VLS) in a silo on the foredeck. Basic missile data: weight 82 kg, length 1.9 m, wingspan 56 cm, range c.56 km, warhead 13.4 kg. The VLS missile is basically similar but has jettisonable tandem boost rocket motors.

Air Launched Missiles

Sea Skua

A small anti-ship missile developed by British Aerospace arming the Lynx helicopters carried by various frigates and destroyers. The missile weighs 147 kg, has a length of 2.85 m and a span of 62 cm. Powered by solid fuel booster and sustainer rocket motors, it has a range of over 15 km at high subsonic speed. Sea Skua is particularly effective against patrol vessels and fast attack craft, as was demonstrated in both the Falklands and Gulf Wars.

Sidewinder

This is one of the world's most successful short range air to air missiles. The AIM-9L version carried by Harriers uses a heat seeking infra red guidance system and has a range of 18 km. Powered by a solid fuel rocket motor boosting it to speeds of Mach 2.5, it weighs 86.6 kg and is 2.87 m long

Guns

114mm Vickers Mk8

The Royal Navy's standard medium calibre general purpose gun which arms the later Type 22s, Type 23 frigates and Type 42 destroyers. A new electrically operated version, the Mod 1, recognised by its angular turret, was introduced in 2001 and will be fitted in the Type 23, Type 22, some Type 42 and the Type 45 classes. Rate of fire: 25 rounds/min. Range: 22,000 m. Weight of Shell: 21 kg.

Goalkeeper

A highly effective automatic Close in Weapons System (CIWS) designed to shoot down missiles and aircraft which have evaded the outer layers of a ships defences. The complete system, designed and built in Holland, is on an autonomous mounting and includes radars, fire control computers and a 7-barrel 30 mm Gatling gun firing 4200 rounds/min. Goalkeeper is designed to engage targets between 350 and 1500 metres away.

Phalanx

A US built CIWS designed around the Vulcan 20 mm rotary cannon. Rate of fire is 3000 rounds/min and effective range is c.1500 m. Fitted in Type 42 destroyers, ARK ROYAL, OCEAN and the Fort Victoria class.

DS30B 30mm

Single 30mm mounting carrying an Oerlikon 30mm gun. Fitted to Type 23 frigates and various patrol vessels and MCMVs. In August 2005 it was announced that the DS30B fitted in Type 23 frigates was to be upgraded to DS30M Mk 2 to include new direct-drive digital servos and the replacement of the earlier Oerlikon KCB cannon with the ATK Mk 44 Bushmaster II 30 mm gun. Consideration is already being given to purchasing additional DS30M Mk 2 systems for minor war vessels and auxiliaries.

GAM BO 20mm

A simple hand operated mounting carrying a single Oerlikon KAA 200 automatic cannon firing 1000 rounds/min. Maximum range is 2000 m. Carried by most of the fleet's major warships except the Type 23 frigates.

20mm Mk.7A

The design of this simple but reliable weapon dates back to World War II but it still provides a useful increase in firepower, particularly for auxiliary vessels and RFAs. Rate of fire 500-800 rounds/min.

Close Range Weapons

In addition to the major weapons systems, all RN ships carry a variety of smaller calibre weapons to provide protection against emerging terrorist threats in port and on the high seas such as small fast suicide craft. In addition it is sometimes preferable, during policing or stop and search operations to have a smaller calibre weapon available. Depending upon the operational environment ships may be seen armed with varying numbers of pedestal mounted General Purpose Machine Guns (GPMG). Another addition to the close in weapons is the Mk 44 Mini Gun a total of 150 of which have been procured from the United States as a fleetwide fit. Fitted to a naval post mount, the Minigun is able to fire up to 3,000 rounds per minute, and is fully self-contained (operating off battery power).

Torpedoes

Stingray

A lightweight anti submarine torpedo which can be launched from ships, helicopters or aircraft. In effect it is an undersea guided missile with a range of 11 km at 45 knots or 7.5 km at 60 knots. Length 2.1 m, diameter 330 mm. Aboard Type 42s and Type 22s Stingray is fired from triple tubes forming part of the Ships Torpedo Weapon System (STWS) but the newer Type 23s have the Magazine Torpedo Launch System (MTLS) with internal launch tubes. Sting Ray Mod 1 is intended to prosecute the same threats as the original Sting Ray but with an enhanced capability against small conventionally powered submarines and an improved shallow-water performance.

Spearfish

Spearfish is a submarine-launched heavyweight torpedo which has replaced Tigerfish. Claimed by the manufacturers to be the world's fastest torpedo, capable of over 70 kts, its sophisticated guidance system includes an onboard acoustic processing suite and tactical computer backed up by a command and control wire link to the parent submarine. Over 20ft in length and weighing nearly two tons, Spearfish is fired from the standard 21-inch submarine torpedo tube and utilises an advanced bi-propellant gas turbine engine for higher performance.

At the end of the line ...

Readers may well find other warships afloat which are not mentioned in this book. The majority have fulfilled a long and useful life and are now relegated to non-seagoing duties. The following list gives details of their current duties:

Pennant No	Ship	Remarks
	BRITANNIA	Ex Royal Yacht at Leith. Open to the public.
	CAROLINE	RNR Drill Ship at Belfast, Northern Ireland.
A134	RAME HEAD	Escort Maintenance Vessel - ex-Royal Marines Training Ship at Portsmouth for disposal.
M29	BRECON	Hunt Class Minehunter - Attached to the New Entry Training Establishment, HMS RALEIGH, Torpoint, as a static Seamanship Training ship.
M103	CROMER	Single Role Minehunter - Attached to Britannia Royal Naval College, Dartmouth as a Static Trainer.
L3505	SIR TRISTRAM	Ex RFA LSL - Refitted as a Static Range Vessel at Portland.
C35	BELFAST	World War II Cruiser Museum ship - Pool of London. Open to the public daily. Tel: 020 7940 6300
D23	BRISTOL	Type 82 Destroyer - Sea Cadet Training Ship at Portsmouth.
D73 S17	CAVALIER OCELOT	World War II Destroyer & Oberon class Submarine Museum Ships at Chatham. Open to the public. Tel: 01634 823800
F126 M1115	PLYMOUTH BRONINGTON	With the withdrawal of their berthing facilities at Birkenhead, Wirral, the ships are closed to the public. The ships remain at Birkenhead whilst discussions over their future continue.
S21	ONYX	At Barrow awaiting public display at proposed Submarine Heritage Centre.

Pennant No	Ship	Remarks
S50	COURAGEOUS	Nuclear-powered Submarine - On display at Devonport Naval Base. Can be visited during Base Tours. Visit Royal Navy website or Tel: 01752 553941 for details.
S67	ALLIANCE	Submarine - Museum Ship at Gosport Open to the public daily. Tel: 023 92 511349
M1151	IVESTON	Static Sea Cadet Training Vessel (Thurrock)

At the time of publishing (December 2008) the following ships were laid up in long term storage or awaiting sale.

PORTSMOUTH: Invincible, Newcastle; Glasgow; Cottesmore; Dulverton; Leeds Castle; Dumbarton Castle; Oakleaf; Brambleleaf; Grey Rover.

PLYMOUTH: Superb; Splendid; Spartan; Sovereign; Conqueror; Valiant; Warspite.

ROSYTH: Resolution; Renown; Repulse; Revenge; Swiftsure; Churchill; Dreadnought.